SOME SURVIVE, TRIUMPH OVER TEARS

A true story of a teenage Mom breaking free from domestic abuse and fighting for the life she wanted for herself and her children.

By
Sharon Wahl

Published by: Book Writing Founders
www.bookwritingfounders.com

ABOUT THE AUTHOR

S haron is, first and foremost, a survivor. She has been married to her soul mate and best friend, John, since 1986. They have three adult children, some grand dogs, and several businesses together. She loves being a wife and mother, interior decorating, cooking, baking, dancing, traveling, snow skiing and water skiing, reading and helping others. Sharon has found her passion in writing and presenting her inspirational messages to groups of many sizes.

For more information on how to book speaking engagements you can visit www.Sharonawahl.com

DEDICATION

I dedicate this book to my family and friends.

It took a community to help my daughters and me survive the dark days of domestic abuse and all the other challenges life has thrown at me.

I also dedicate this book to all the unborn children that never got to live, including my own.

My final dedication is to all those who work to protect anyone from abuse of any kind, especially women and children.

ACKNOWLEDGEMENTS

It is by the amazing grace of God that I survived all the trauma and am alive today to write this book. I cannot fully express the amount of gratitude I have for my loving and devoted parent's Donald and Lois Graham who shared their faith in God with me all my life and never gave up on me, even as a rebel teenager. Many times, my parents and siblings, Donny, Joyce, Mark, Kathleen, Janice, Doris, Scott, and Neil came to rescue Jennifer and I when we were in danger and welcomed us home. I could not have gone back to school or worked without the countless hours of babysitting that my family, mainly my mother, sisters and friends Kathi Schemm and Joanne Jester provided. For any other babysitters I am forgetting to name, thank you.

A special thank you Cardinal Dan DiNardo, the late Manny Manolias and Carol Westwood who all provided counseling and support to a broken spirit that needed the love, wisdom and healing they provided.

My loving remembrance for the late Mrs. Elizabeth Duncan for her loving guidance and support while going through the adoption process and picking the right family for my daughter.

For all my dear friends that have prayed for me, encouraged me, and read drafts of my book for me, thank you! And finally, I want to acknowledge the unconditional love, support, understanding and constant encouragement from my husband John Wahl and our amazing adult children, Jennifer, Sarah, and David and our daughter in laws, Maggie and Lindsay, while writing and rewriting this book. They have loved me unconditionally, read many drafts of this book and encouraged me to share my story and never give up.

I hope that in sharing this painful journey I may help someone else on their journey to not only survive, but to triumph over tears.

INTRODUCTION

I never expected many of the trials and hardships that I experienced during my lifetime. You may feel the same way. You may have heard the saying, "What doesn't kill you makes you stronger." That is kind of how I got my nickname, "Superwoman." The nickname started when I was going through a difficult period in my life, and I made the Alicia Keys song "Superwoman" the ringtone on my phone. Ironically, my initials are S.W. Then my husband, John, made the name stick with a life-size, carved wooden statue of Superwoman with my face on it.

I can assure you I have felt like anything other than a Superwoman, but I am now a strong woman, having survived much adversity, and I feel empowered!

I share in this book my deepest regrets and some painful experiences to help women of all ages know that they are not alone and that there is hope and healing available.

I credit my strength and healing to my faith in a higher power I call God, the support of my family and my sheer determination to have the life I wanted, not a life of pain and misery. I am a Christian and believe in Jesus Christ. You may not believe in God or a Higher Power. Whatever you believe or wherever you are on this journey we call life is OK. Life is a journey, not a destination. However, we are all on the journey together whether we like it or not. What we do and what we say matters. Our words and actions have power, and that is one of the reasons I am writing this book.

I have learned so many valuable lessons, unfortunately, many the hard way. I have known love and heartache, success and failure, health and illness. I am sharing with you the good, the bad and the ugly. It has taken me years to truly love and forgive myself for decisions I regret making, but I have finally found inner peace.

One of my favorite quotes by Ralph Waldo Emerson hangs framed in my office of a beautiful ocean scene with the turquoise water washing up on the sand and a rainbow in the sky. It says, "What lies before us and what lies behind us are tiny matters compared to what lies within us." This book was in me, and it needed to be written. What lies within you?

CONTENTS

chapter 1

I'm Late

~

"I really think a champion is defined not by their wins but how they can recover when they fall."

Serena Williams

E very woman that has ever been late for her period knows that it means she could be pregnant. Ever since I started having periods at age eleven, my body had been like clockwork. Every twenty-eight days, I would get my period. I was just two days late and I was freaking out. If my periods were not regular, I would not have been so concerned. The first problem was that I was only fourteen and a freshman in high school. The second problem was that I had been sneaking around all summer with my boyfriend, who turned nineteen in August. Earlier in the summer, my parents found out how old my new boyfriend was, and they forbade me to see him anymore.

We met earlier that year in late spring when I went to an under 21 dance club with a couple of my girlfriends. I think you had to be 16 or 18 to get in, but we dressed up with lots of makeup and did our hair to look older and we got in. We may have had an ID from one of our older sisters, but one way or another, we were determined to get into that dance club because we loved to dance, and there were guys there. My lipstick was dark, and my eye makeup made my blue eyes pop. There was no way I looked like I was fourteen and still in eighth grade. I was supposed to meet Rickie, a guy I had a huge crush on, but I wasn't going to stand around waiting.

While I was dancing with my friends, I could see this very handsome, muscular guy with dark hair and beautiful hazel eyes watching me. Several girls were hanging around him and talking to him, but he kept watching me. Soon, I found out his name was Lenny. I kept an eye on the door waiting for Rickie to show up, but he never did. Toward the end of the night, I went over to be with my friends when Lenny and I started talking. Since we had some mutual friends, we decided that we would meet up at some point, and I think I gave him my phone number. There were no cell phones, so it would have been my home phone number.

I knew Lenny had his own apartment and that he was in the Marines briefly. I had also heard he had a rough childhood and that his father had been abusive but was no longer living. His mom had been married a couple of other times, but Lenny never got along with his stepfathers, and that was one of the reasons he was living on his own at such a young age. His life sounded nothing like mine. My parents were still happily married, and I lived in the same house I grew up in with them and my eight siblings. I am the youngest of five girls and have two older and two younger brothers.

I used to be very athletic and was involved in basketball and cheerleading until June 7th, 1976, when I was put on limited physical activity by a cardiologist for having a heart murmur. I was devastated being taken away from all my friends and healthy activities, but I wasn't given a choice. I acted like it didn't bother me, but it did bother me that I could not be in cheerleading with my friends. Deep down, I was angry about it. I became rebellious and more of a rule breaker than a follower. I loved school, but I was different than I used to be. It would have been better for me to stay in sports than start hanging out with older friends that smoked and drank.

Once I met Lenny, we spent a lot of time together when he wasn't at work doing various odd jobs, including installing carpets. I usually told my parents I was with my girlfriends or at the swimming pool. At some point over the summer, Lenny started pressuring me to have sex with him. I was still a virgin and was raised believing that you were supposed to wait till you got married to have sex. I was kind of terrified of having sex even though I liked kissing him and liked all the attention he gave me. He continued to work on me, telling me that he was a virgin too and that if I loved him, we should make love. I thought I loved him, and eventually, I gave in to his pressure.

We were at his tiny apartment on his single bed when we had sex for the first time. I don't remember it being very memorable, and I did not understand why people made such a big deal about how great sex was. That was until we spent more time exploring each other's bodies and having sex on a regular basis. I think we used condoms and counted days of the month, staying away from the middle of the month when I would be ovulating and more fertile. We were not very smart, and I was not making the best decisions at the time.

One Saturday, I was helping my mother clean our house as we usually did on Saturdays when I started having severe abdominal pains. I sometimes had painful periods, but this did not seem normal. My Dad drove me to Central Medical Hospitals ER so I could be seen there.

I was examined by the Doctor, and they did some tests. After what seemed like forever, the Doctor came back into my room and told me that I had an infection in my ovaries and that I would probably not be able to have children. He reassured me that he was not going to tell my father that I was sexually active. A nurse came in and gave me a couple of shots of antibiotics, and they sent me home. For some reason, I did not tell my mother or father that the Doctor said I might not be able to have children. But I did tell Lenny. We thought this meant we could have sex as much as we wanted and not have to worry about getting pregnant. That was pretty much what we did. We had unprotected sex all the time.

So that was how I got to this point of being late for my period. I was now class President at an all-female Catholic High School, and I needed a pregnancy test. Home pregnancy tests were not popular yet, and I had no idea how to find out if I was pregnant without my parents finding out. I must have used the yellow page's phone book to call Planned Parenthood to find out how to get a pregnancy test. To my surprise, I had to bring in my first morning urine and keep it cold for them to be able to test for the pregnancy hormones. The problem with that plan was I was in high School, and Lenny and I did not have a car. I also had the problem of keeping it cold. I was able to collect my first morning urine in a clean peanut butter jar and sneak it into my backpack. After walking over a mile to school, I was able to go to my friend Karen's house right behind our school and keep it in her refrigerator in a brown paper bag until after school.

I then had to collect the bag from the refrigerator and hop on a bus to downtown Pittsburgh after school and get to Planned Parenthood to get the pregnancy test. This process took a long time, and even though I was over two weeks late, the pregnancy test was negative. By the time I left the clinic, it was dark outside. I was pretty sure the test was wrong because, besides being late for my period, my breasts were tender and they had visibly grown in size. Planned Parenthood gave me a bag of condoms and sent me on my way. I got home so late that my family was having dinner. I ditched the condoms before I walked into the house and had to make up some crazy story about where I was and why I was so late.

I tried to carry on like everything was fine, but deep down, I was pretty sure I was, in fact, pregnant. The biggest problem I had was trying to figure out how I was going to get back down to Planned Parenthood and do it all over again.

By the time I was able to get back to Planned Parenthood for another Pregnancy test, it was December, and it was cold outside. I was able to save some time by hiding my first morning urine in the bushes outside of school instead of going to Karen's house. This time I had Lenny and another friend Kathi go with me. I had missed three periods and was fully expecting the test to be positive. We entered a large room filled with lots of chairs and signed in on a clipboard at a glass window.

At one point, a lady came and collected my urine sample returning shortly after with a postcard that she handed to me. It read, the pregnancy test performed today, with the date filled in, on Sharon Graham, had a checkmark next to the word POSITIVE. I took the card and left Planned Parenthood, not quite sure how to break the news to my parents. I knew the news that their 14-year-old daughter was pregnant was going to be very upsetting, especially since my dad had just been in the hospital for some type of irregular heartbeat.

I called my mom and asked her if Lenny and I could come and talk with her. She probably thought I wanted to talk to her about dating him, not to tell her that I had been having sex with him and that I was pregnant.

When Lenny and I got to my house, my mom was sitting alone in our living room in a rocking chair with one lamp on. I didn't say anything I just walked over and handed her the postcard that said I was pregnant. I think she was in shock. The first words out of her mouth were, "how many periods have you missed?" I think she was further in shock when I said three. She repeated what I said out loud, "three!" I don't remember much more other than she told Lenny to leave. I guess I felt some relief not having this huge secret anymore. My mom did say that she had no idea how she was going to break this news to my dad and that she wanted to speak to his doctor before she told him. His doctor advised that she wait until after Christmas and until his medication was working to regulate his heartbeat to tell him I was pregnant. Honestly, I have no idea how she was able to keep it together and act like nothing was different throughout the holiday season.

You would think I would remember sitting down with my parents and having a conversation about what was going to happen, but I don't remember that. I always knew I was having my baby and keeping my baby, even if I had no idea how that was going to happen. I believed I was in love with Lenny and that one day we would get married. I had no idea how young I was; that didn't register in my brain. I do know that my parents could have pressed charges against Lenny because I was a minor and he was nineteen years old, even though I said it was consensual and that I loved him. It may have had something to do with the fact that my mother met my dad when she was fourteen and he was three years older than her. She was crazy about him at fourteen and accepted his engagement ring at sixteen before he left for the Navy for three years. I don't know if that influenced their decision to not press charges against him, but they did forbid me to see him.

I was no longer going to attend St. Elizabeth Ann Seton High School for the remainder of my freshman year. My parents found a facility funded through the Catholic Church that would allow me to live there during the week and have private tutor's come in and teach my classes and allow me to go home on the weekends. It was on the other side of town, and Lenny did not know where I was so this was their way of keeping me away from Lenny and helping me stay in school. Besides the regular classes I was taking, like typing and Algebra, they offered natural childbirth classes and parenting classes.

The place was called Rosalia Manor, and it was a big old mansion with lots of large windows, carved wood, cool staircases, and French doors to outside patios. The first floor had many of the large rooms converted into classrooms, along with the large dining room where we had our meals and the large kitchen where we helped to prep meals and clean up. The second floor had offices for counselors and our lounge area, and the third floor had lots of bedrooms and bathrooms for the residents. It was a beautiful place, and I was treated very well there, but I still got homesick at times and couldn't wait to get home on the weekends.

On one of my weekends home, my mother brought up the subject of adoption for me to consider. I told her there was absolutely no way I would be able to give my baby up for adoption. I was 100% certain I was having my baby and keeping the baby.

She asked me what I planned to do if my father was not supportive of me living there once the baby came, and I told her I would figure it out. I had already gone to the welfare office to apply for assistance. I would need money for formula, diapers, and medical coverage for the baby. After I made my intentions clear to my parents and my family that I was having and keeping my baby, they were very supportive and helped in more ways than I could have imagined. My mom became my Lamaze coach and went to all the childbirth classes with me. She had given birth ten times and never saw a baby be born. The birth of my baby was the first time she witnessed a baby being born. That was a very special bond she would always have with Jennifer and me.

When I was closer to my due date, my parents surprised me on one of the weekends I came home. They had the little bedroom I would share with the baby painted light yellow and a new carpet installed. Someone had given me a crib with sheets and all kinds of things I would need for the baby. They had the bedroom all set up for the baby. My mom had a changing table she had used for my youngest brother and lots of receiving blankets and baby clothes. I was excited about becoming a mother even though I was so young. I had a great mother and always knew one day I wanted to be a mother. I just had no idea how young I was.

My pregnancy was progressing along normally, and I was finishing up my classes while getting closer to my due date, which was June 27th. I had not seen or spoken to Lenny for a long time because my parents wanted me to stay away from him, and Lenny did not know how to contact me. That was until one day I was walking to a local corner store out by Rosalia when I heard a male voice calling my name. It was Lenny. He had been walking the streets of Oakland trying to find me for a while. I was kind of happy to see him and kind of terrified at the same time. I loved him and I missed him, but I knew what my parents had been doing for me and my baby and I did not want to hurt them again. Lenny insisted on coming to visit me at Rosalia, and then he convinced me to start meeting up with him. He had such a strong hold on me that I started sneaking around again to see him.

On June 6th, we made plans to meet up at his apartment. Since I was already pregnant, we didn't need to worry about me getting pregnant and surprisingly, I was still able to enjoy sex. After we made love, Lenny decided he was going to make us rigatoni for lunch. While he was cooking, I started having very strong contractions. I could tell they were real because my diaphragm muscle was getting hard and pressing down so intense I could feel it in my vagina. When I told Lenny I was in labor and could not eat lunch, he did not believe me and was kind of mad at me for not eating what he had prepared. I told him I had to leave because I had to get back to Rosalia, which meant taking a streetcar into town and a bus to Oakland while in labor. I did not want my parents to know I was with him. By the time I got to the hospital, I was already five centimeters dilated and shortly after arriving, my water broke. My mom arrived at the hospital to be my coach, and we thought it was going to be quick, but around midnight, my contractions stopped.

My doctor was running around Magee Women's Hospital delivering other babies and wanted to see if my contractions would start again on their own without Pitocin to induce my labor. I had not eaten since breakfast on June 6th and it was now June 7th, and I was not allowed to have anything but ice chips and lollypops. I felt bad my labor was taking so long because it was my younger brother Scott's birthday, and our mother was with me all day, but I was about to give him a birthday gift of a niece or nephew born on his birthday. I was so hungry and so tired that I fell asleep for a bit. At some point, Lenny showed up at the Hospital. My Parents could not keep him from seeing me at the hospital, but my mother would not allow him to be in the delivery room. If I remember correctly, he had been celebrating with his friends and had been drinking and smelled like alcohol. That did not go over well at all.

Finally, around 3 pm, they gave me medication to restart my labor, and at 10:33 pm, I gave birth to my precious, healthy baby girl, Jennifer Marie. She was twenty days early but still weighed six pounds. She was perfect, with all her fingers and toes, and absolutely gorgeous with her sweet little mouth and dimples. She had bluish-green eyes, long eyelashes, soft brown baby hair and she was mine. Once I saw her and held her in my arms, I could feel a massive amount of responsibility for her coming over me. I was hungry, exhausted and very happy the nurses were there to take care of Jennifer and me because I needed some food and some sleep.

At first, I was petrified. I had read about postpartum depression, but I didn't realize that it would make me an emotional mess for several days. There were so many changes going on with my body. I had stitches from the episiotomy done to prevent tearing during childbirth. My abdomen had stretch marks, despite all the cream I rubbed on while pregnant to prevent them, and on day three, when my milk came in, I looked like Dolly Parton. I was not going to be breastfeeding, and my doctor would not give me the shot to dry up my milk. He had me tightly wrap towels around my chest to help stop the production of milk. Without air conditioning and the heat of June, the milk-soaked towels smelled like sour milk. I did not really mind, though because I was in love with my adorable baby girl, Jennifer.

She was my daughter, and I was going to be the best mother I could be to her. Although my family was not expecting their 15-year-old to have a baby, they welcomed her with loving arms and hearts.

My parents still had five kids at home, and Jennifer blended right in with the rest of us. On the way home from the hospital, my mom turned the radio on and said, "we might as well get her used to the noise." Even though I was only fifteen years old, I was a good mom because I had a great mom, and I knew how to take care of a baby. I'm always thankful for that. Plus, I had lots of help from my parents, siblings, and friends. My youth was stolen, but I got one of the greatest gifts of my life in exchange, my daughter Jennifer. I cannot imagine my life without her.

My youngest brother, Neil, was only five when Jennifer was born, so he was delighted to welcome her to our family. He was her uncle, but they were more like brother and sister than Uncle and niece. He loved to hold her and give her a bottle. He couldn't wait until they could play together. He was such a big help running to grab me a diaper or just making her smile and coo. Jennifer was such a sweet baby, and we were all making it work.

Over the summer, my family and I were adjusting to having a new baby in the house. I could not afford to use pampers, so I had to wash cloth diapers, and since I chose not to breastfeed, I had to mix formula and make bottles. Lenny just started coming around once Jennifer was born, and I guess my parents felt they could not really stop him from seeing his baby. There was a lot of tension in the house when he was around, but we were all trying to make the best of the situation. I loved taking Jennifer on long walks in her stroller, taking her to our local swimming pool and spending every minute I could with her before I headed back to high school in the fall. Lenny had been working steady and had enough money to buy a car, a cream-colored Camaro. When we were together, he was kind of controlling and jealous of the time Jennifer took away from him. Lenny also did not want me to go back to high School.

My mother, after raising nine of her own children, offered to take care of my 3-month-old baby, Jennifer, so I could go back to high school as a sophomore. I wanted to go and was excited about it. I would be going to a new public high school. Brashear was a huge school with about 3000 students consisting of two buildings, the North house and the South house.

Lenny was very vocal with me about him not wanting me to go back to High School. He liked to control me, and he was making it sound like High School was a waste of my time. Like I didn't need the education. He was jealous of anything and everything in my life that wasn't him. He was like a large, spoiled child that needed attention all the time. He had become more insecure and demanding. I was going back to school, and he was furious. He needed me to need him and did not want me to be out of his sight.

One day when we were at his apartment, he kind of shocked me. I think we were talking about me going back to school, but he got mad and pushed me. I fell backward over his weights that were on the floor. I was not injured; just kind of shocked. That was the first time he ever did anything like that. Later he apologized to me and said he had no idea why he did that, and he would never do anything like that again. I let it go but it was a red flag that I should not have ignored. I had no idea what he was capable of.

chapter 2

Prince Charming is Not So Charming

" Trauma may happen to you, but it can never define you. "

Melinda Longtin

G oing back to school with an infant daughter was certainly not easy. I would go to school most of the day, come home, make bottles with formula, wash and fold diapers, take care of my daughter, do homework and in the evenings, Lenny would come to visit. Usually, I would get to bed around 11 pm. Then I had to wake up around 4 am to feed Jennifer and hopefully get her back to sleep quickly, then get up about 5 am to shower and eat before I caught my school bus at 6 am to start the day all over with my high school classes. It was taking a toll on me as I was not getting enough rest.

My family was not happy about me seeing Lenny, but they had given up on the idea of keeping us apart. Lenny did not hide his feelings about me going back to high school, so that created even more tension in our house.

I was taking my normal classes and sewing as an elective. A September sewing assignment was to purchase some fabric and other items needed to make a blouse. On September 26, 1979, my mom and Jennifer and I just arrived home from the fabric store after purchasing what I needed for the sewing class.

Earlier that afternoon, I ran into my old crush Rickie, the guy who didn't show up the night I met Lenny. During my lunch break, Rickie and I sat outside and talked for a little while. Somehow word got back to Lenny that I had been sitting and talking with Rickie. Being the very jealous and controlling person Lenny was, my conversation with Rickie at lunch made him extremely angry. He didn't want me back in School, and one of the reasons was he couldn't control me there.

It was probably around 8 pm, close to getting dark when Lenny pulled up in front of our house in his cream-colored Camaro. I did not know anything about him being upset when he arrived. I had taken Jennifer out of her car seat and walked down our front steps to the car to say hello and talk to him. I opened the car door and sat on the front seat with Jennifer in my arms, and I could tell he was agitated. He began yelling at me for talking to Rickie at lunch, like I had done something wrong. We were just talking.

Lenny pulled away from my parent's house and sped up the street yelling at me and blowing the whole thing out of proportion. I had never seen him like this before. Nothing I said could calm him down or make a difference in what he perceived as a threat. I didn't have my seatbelt on, and I didn't have Jennifer in her car seat. Lenny reached over and grabbed Jennifer out of my arms while he was driving at a high speed, racing down Pioneer Avenue. I began yelling at him to stop and give me the baby screaming, "what are you doing, you are going to hurt her!" I was pleading for him to give her back to me and to stop the car. I was afraid he was going to crash the car and hurt her. I tried to grab her from him, and he backhanded me with his fist right in my face.

I could not believe he hit me. He had never hit me before. I could not believe this was happening. I tried to grab Jennifer again, and he hit me again. I tried several times, and he repeatedly backhanded me with his fist in my face. At this point, my lips were swollen, my nose was bleeding, my eyes were bruised, and Jennifer was crying hysterically. He took me to a dark street I didn't know and was saying something about killing me and my parents reading about it in the newspaper. In my horror and disbelief, I was praying for this nightmare to stop. I just wanted to be home with Jennifer and be safe.

I could not believe that this was the person that I loved, the father of my child who had turned on me, on us. I was sobbing at this point, and he finally gave Jennifer back to me. I was holding her in my arms, trying to comfort her. Lenny began to calm down and drove toward his apartment. I was terrified and had no idea what was going to happen. As he was driving along slowly on Broadway Avenue, pulling up close to his apartment, I opened the door, jumped out of the car, and started running with Jennifer in my arms. He stopped the car and ran after me. He caught up to us quickly and when he did, he swung me around by one arm and punched me in my face with a full fist sending both of us flying through the air. I landed on a concrete sidewalk on my back and Jennifer, 3 ½ months old, landed on my chest and rolled into the street.

When I sat up to grab her, my nose gushed blood all over both of us. I started running again with her in my arms to a neighbor's house and pounding on the door screaming for help. The man that opened the door will never forget my face for as long as he lives. Lenny was trying to pull Jennifer from my arms. I was holding her tightly so Lenny could not take her from me again.

The man at the door said, "let her go, you're going to hurt her," so I let go and Lenny took off with her in the car, leaving me hysterical, bruised, and bloody. I later learned that the man that answered the door was a fireman.

After a brief while, my dad and several police cars arrived. Lenny pulled up in his car and someone brought Jennifer back to me. After Jennifer was back in my arms, it took four police officers and my father to get Lenny to the ground and handcuff him and arrest him because he was resisting. After filing a police report, I was taken to the emergency room and treated for my injuries. Amazingly, Jennifer was physically unharmed. I believe I was in shock. I looked like I had just done a couple of rounds in the boxing ring with Rocky. I stayed home from school long enough to let the bruises heal and then went back to school.

It would be several months before the case for domestic abuse would be heard in court. By the time we were scheduled for court, the physical signs of the beating were long healed. Lenny constantly sent flowers, cards, and gifts and apologized continuously, saying how sorry he was and how it would never happen again. I wanted to believe him because I was still in love with him, and we had a baby girl and I thought I could fix him.

Lenny agreed to go to counseling to our family priest, Father DiNardo. I wanted to give him a chance to redeem himself.

By the time there was a court date and against the advice of the police and my parents, I dropped the charges against Lenny. My family was furious that I would give Lenny another chance after what he had done to Jennifer and me. I was too young and confused to be making adult decisions at fifteen years old. As you can imagine, this created a huge amount of tension at home between my family, Lenny and me.

I was tired of sneaking around trying to see Lenny, and he convinced me that I did not have to listen to my parents anymore. On January 4, 1980, when my parents were out, I packed up mine and Jennifer's belongings, and we moved into Lenny's hole-in-the-wall apartment to be a little family. I didn't even realize that it was my mother's birthday; that's how self-absorbed and mixed up I was. Lenny had managed to turn me against the family that I had loved all my life.

Everything my family had done for us, and I wasn't thinking about anything other than what I wanted. That January, I signed myself out of high school and officially became a high school dropout, playing Suzie homemaker in our shoebox apartment. To say our apartment was an efficiency would be generous. It literally was a long rectangle that could only fit a single bed, which we shared. The bed doubled as our sofa, and we barely had room for a portable crib. In the kitchen area we had a little round table with two chairs and just enough room for Jennifer's highchair. We only had a shower stall, no tub, so I had to bath Jennifer in the kitchen sink. I didn't mind because we were together and that is what we wanted. I made the best of the situation.

My parents did talk to a social worker about trying to make me come home because I was still a minor, but they were told I could legally emancipate myself. I'm sure that was not what they wanted to hear. I can't even imagine how sick with worry they must have been. Lenny promised me he would never hurt me again. I thought he was going to be a good father to Jennifer and, someday, my husband. I wanted to be able to have a happy family like the one I grew up in and nothing like the one he grew up in.

Lenny was no longer installing carpet for his friend Tom. He had gotten into the Ironworkers Union. When he worked, he made good money, but ironworkers move around a lot and get laid off often. They work on bridges and buildings, so in winter months, there are more layoffs. When Lenny was at work, I cleaned the apartment, took care of Jennifer, and prepared meals. We hadn't been living together very long, just over a month when Lenny broke his promise to not get violent again. I was preparing dinner and had the table all set with the dishes and silverware. I had put the corn and chicken I had made on the table because I was expecting Lenny any minute. Jennifer was asleep in her portable crib. Lenny came home, and I realized that he had been drinking. I inquired about his mood and why he was so upset. He began yelling at me about money and told me that he had gotten laid off that day. Things escalated quickly, and he flipped the table sending all the dishes and food flying everywhere. I stood by the kitchen door, terrified, unable to move. I had not witnessed anything like this growing up. My dad treated my mother with respect. He never swore and especially not at her. As I stood there, frozen, Lenny picked up a large carving knife and threw it at me.

I could not believe he had thrown a knife at me. The knife just missed my face and stuck right in the door frame right beside my eyeball. Surprisingly, Jennifer was still sound asleep, and I knew he would not hurt her. I opened that door and took off running like a bat out of hell. I did not stop running until I got to my sister Kathleen's apartment, several blocks away. I was pounding on the door, screaming, "let me in, let me in."

My sister, Kathleen, called my two older brothers, Donny and Mark and told them what had happened. My brothers picked up a very muscular friend of theirs also named Mark, on the way to my apartment to assist them with going to get Jennifer. My brothers already disliked Lenny for what he had done to me and now they were even more upset about what had just happened. When they arrived to collect Jennifer, Lenny did not want to let them into the apartment. They had to break the window to unlock the door and get inside, but they were not leaving there without 8-month-old Jennifer, who miraculously slept through the whole incident.

Under such duress, my parents welcomed us back into their home. I know my parents had been worried sick about Jennifer and me and were keeping our safety and protection in their prayers.

I believe there was a divine intervention around us because Jennifer or I could have been killed in either of these incidents. It still amazes me that my nose was not broken from that direct punch to my face or my back broken as hard as I hit the cement while clinging to my infant daughter, and she remained unharmed from rolling into the street and no cars were coming. In the second incident, a knife hurled at me just missed my face. If you ask me if I believe in Guardian Angels, the answer is most definitely Yes! Regrettably, the roller coaster ride from hell with Lenny was far from over.

chapter 3

My Not So Sweet 16

~

"It is not the bruises on the body that hurt. It is the   wounds of the heart and the scars on the mind."

Aisha Warrier

I had moved back home after the knife incident and was trying to carry on with my life, but Lenny would not leave me alone. Back then, there was no such thing as caller ID., and the only way to tell who was calling was to answer the phone.

Lenny would call constantly apologizing, crying, saying how much he loved me and that he would never hurt me again. He said he was drunk when he threw the knife at me, he just got laid off, he was worried about financially supporting us, and on and on.

Lenny was like an addiction to me. Just like an alcoholic or drug addict, I kept going back to him, even though it was dangerous. When he was good, he was charming and handsome and knew how to get to me. He would show up looking and smelling good, knowing that I still had feelings for him and promising we could still be a happy family.

He was steadily working as an iron worker and back to working on me to come back to him again. He had moved into a nice, two-bedroom apartment on Los Angeles Avenue. He wanted to show me the apartment, and he wanted me to help him pick furniture and decorate it. I love to decorate, and it comes easily to me, so I was excited to help him.

It was a cute second-floor apartment with a large, equipped kitchen and a pretty bathroom with a shower and bathtub with nice ceramic tiles, nothing like the dumpy bachelor pad he had before. We picked new bedroom and living room furniture and hung curtains and pictures. His mom and third stepfather helped with small appliances for the kitchen and dishes. We decorated the second bedroom for Jennifer with the Sesame Street theme. It was so cute. I think my family knew that it was inevitable that Jennifer and I were going to move into that apartment with him and try to start over again. It was shortly after my sixteenth birthday, and this time, I was certain things were going to be better. I was hoping we both had learned some valuable lessons, and Lenny worked so hard to get us back.

When Lenny was working as an Iron Worker, I was home more with Jennifer, cooking, cleaning up and taking care of Jennifer. It would have been perfect if Lenny didn't always have to be so controlling. He was so jealous of everything and everyone. The more he isolated me and kept me from my friends and family, the more he could control me.

For example, he would not let me go to the store to get cigarettes without him. He would accuse me of flirting with other men or checking them out. His behavior was unpredictable and often inappropriate for the situation.

One night we had friends over and were playing a card game at the kitchen table. I do not remember what I said or did that set him off, but he took his glass of beer and threw it in my face. Of course, an argument followed. At times he was just mean and nasty.

When Lenny found out I was on the birth control pill, he was angry with me and crushed them. He took his one arm and cleared off everything on my dresser onto the floor, including a jewelry box and perfume bottles. There was broken glass everywhere. I thought that maybe he wanted me to be pregnant, so he could further control me, and I couldn't leave him. I never knew which Lenny he was going to be. The kind and loving one or the mean and violent one.

Then my period was late, and my breasts were tender. I knew I was pregnant again. Lenny did not want me on birth control, but he was freaking out, saying we could not afford another baby. He went on and on ranting about not being able to have this baby.

I was early in the pregnancy because I had just missed my period, maybe two weeks. Lenny's sister was telling me she had an abortion, like she just had a haircut or something, like it was no big deal. Lenny was pressuring me to have an abortion. Some of my friends and a few other people that I respected that knew about abortion also thought that I was too young to have another baby.

My parents had no idea I was pregnant, but the few people I told were pressuring me to have an abortion, maybe because they were afraid for my safety and Jennifer's safety. I knew in my heart that I didn't want to have an abortion, but I was confused and scared. I had just turned sixteen, and my daughter was just ten months old.

Friends and even medical staff pressuring me said it wasn't a baby yet, that it was just a blob of tissues, and the sooner I did it, the better, the less developed the fetus would be. I rationalized the whole thing. I made myself believe the lies and gave in to the pressure. On May 30th, 1980, I went to the same hospital that delivered my baby girl almost a year earlier and had the abortion. Because I was still on my father's health insurance, my doctor gave me general anesthesia, so I was not awake for the procedure. When I woke up, I was holding my abdomen and crying, knowing that what I did was terribly wrong. The guilt was unbearable.

When Lenny picked me up from the hospital, I asked him to please go into the store to get me the feminine pads I needed because I was bleeding. He gave me such a hard time about getting pads because that was embarrassing to him. I could not believe he would be more concerned about what other people thought than helping take care of me at that time. I hated him for pressuring me to have the abortion. I was so disgusted with myself that I hated myself too. I would have to live with this decision for the rest of my life. That was the beginning of my self-loathing. The next day I called my parents and asked if Jennifer and I could please come home. They said yes, and within an hour, my dad was outside of our apartment, helping me load up our belongings. I wanted to be as far away from Lenny as possible. Jennifer and I moved back to Fordham Avenue again.

I tried to put on a happy face, but my innocence was long gone. Every chance I had to get a babysitter, I would go out with friends to drink myself into oblivion or get high smoking weed to try to numb the pain. I was fortunate to have the family that I had to help me raise my daughter. I tried to give her the happiest childhood I could under the circumstances of our lives. Part of me hated Lenny for forcing me to have that abortion, but I hated myself too for going through with it.

Jennifer was such a charming, sweet, loving, funny little girl. Her soft brown hair had grown to her shoulders with little curls at her neck, her big hazel eyes had a sparkle, and she had deep dimples in her cheeks when she smiled. I know she loved me so much, and I loved her more than life itself. I know that, at times, it was that little girl that needed me and kept me going. I wanted to be better for her, but I was really hurting inside.

Then to make matters worse, my mom got a bill in the mail from the insurance company showing that I had gone into the hospital and had general anesthesia. She looked at me and said, "is this what I think it's for?" She knew what it was for. She didn't judge me; she simply suggested that I go see Father DiNardo and go to confession. I'm sure part of her was heartbroken, and part of her was relieved that I was not with him and was not having another child with him. I did go see Father Dan and go to confession. God may have forgiven me, but I didn't forgive myself and that forgiveness I would not give to myself for many years. I treated myself poorly because I was punishing myself. I was not ok.

A ray of hope showed up when I really needed it. The day was chilly, so I bundled Jennifer up in her pink coat with a hood and went for a walk with her in her stroller. We were walking along Brookline Blvd. when we ran into Joanne, a woman I used to babysit for. She was a manager at Anthony's Curtain Shop, and she asked me if I would be interested in working at the store. I used to watch her daughter and son, and she knew I was a hard worker and because I love interior decorating, I was really excited about possibly working there. My mother offered to babysit so I could accept the job. I think my mother knew I would be good at it and that I needed something to do, and it would help me earn a little extra money. Joanne, my manager, taught me how to help people order custom window treatments and blinds. I got to work on the window displays and was good at it. I loved my job, and I loved meeting people. Joanne was aware of all the troubles I was having with Lenny. She was trying to help me, and it was working. I was gaining some healthy self-esteem.

The next several years were like a roller coaster ride. Lenny turned into a stalker. He would call and harass me regularly. He would show up unannounced at my work, outside my work, and anywhere I went, he would be there. This was before PFA'S (Protection From Abuse Orders) were easily available and I was not really aware of them.

One night I walked up to Brookline Boulevard with Jennifer to Baskin-Robbins to get our favorite ice cream. I ran into my very first boyfriend, Denny, from couple skating at Bethel Park Roller Skating Rink. Denny offered to walk us home because it was getting dark. When we arrived back to my house, it was time for Jennifer to go to bed. My sister Kathleen sat at the dining room table, working on a paper for a class she was taking and typing away. It was a weeknight around 11 PM, and my parents and younger brothers had already gone to bed. The phone kept ringing, but I did not want to answer it because I was pretty sure that it was Lenny calling, and I did not want to talk to him. After a while, the phone went silent, it was sort of nice. But then there was a loud bang, and to our surprise, the front door came flying off the hinges and in burst Lenny in a rage. The wooden door landed in the entrance hallway with another loud bang, and Lenny went after my friend, Denny. I don't remember if he punched or kicked Denny in the face, but Denny's one eye swelled completely shut instantly. Lenny grabbed Denny and dragged him through the broken glass with his shirt over his head. It was instant madness. Everyone in the house was up, and the police were called.

My father was trying to keep Lenny there till the police arrived. I believe someone was trying to drag him over to throw him down the steps. My older brothers no longer lived with us, so my dad was the only adult male except for Denny, who couldn't see and was bleeding. I can't remember everything that happened, but I remember my mother in her nightgown running around saying, "where is a damn baseball bat when you need one!" There was always an aluminum baseball bat down in the corner by the front door and on this insane night, thank God there wasn't because she probably would've killed him. By the time the police arrived, Lenny had taken off in his car. What a mess, complete chaos.

My dad and I pressed charges and had to go to the Magistrate, Charlie McLaughlin. The goal was to get Lenny to pay for my parent's front door and to get him to stay away from us. Denny did come to testify, but he didn't come around anymore after that. I can't say I blamed him.

I started taking classes to get my GED, which is a general education diploma, so that I could go back to college for something and get a good job. On Sept. 4th, 1980, I took the test and passed the first time. I still worked at the curtain shop and loved my job there. I got to be better friends with Joanne and Jane, coworkers that both lived on my street.

My family was afraid for my life because Lenny would not leave me alone. I think they were hoping that if I got out of Pittsburgh for a little bit, that would help to clear my head and protect me from him. My brother Mark and his wife Leanne lived in Norfolk, Virginia, at the time and had just had my nephew Mark Junior on Christmas Eve. I didn't have the money to fly, so my parents helped me out with money for a Greyhound bus ticket to Virginia. It was sometime at the beginning of the year in 1981. I do remember it was before my seventeenth birthday because I just passed the test for driver's permit and was working on getting my license.

I went to Virginia for a week to get away from everything, and, to be honest, I think my family needed a break from all the drama as well. I did feel a sense of relief being away from Pittsburgh and Lenny. His constant harassing was exhausting.

During this time my sister Joyce was going through an unexpected and heartbreaking divorce while pregnant with her second child and working on finishing nursing school. She had to have an emergency cesarean due to placenta previa which is life threatening. Joyce and her son Danny who was 2 months early could have died. Danny was only 4 pounds and rather than have him and her older son Matthew in Daycare she offered to pay me to take care of her boys at her home. We both agreed that having my drivers license would be helpful to both of us, so she took me right around my seventeenth birthday and I passed.

Having my license helped me help Joyce with both of her sons, Matthew and Danny and spend more time with Jennifer. It was good for both of us because I could spend the night when she had early morning classes or clinical rotations. Part of me missed working at the Curtain shop, but I liked the flexibility and being able to help my sister. It was also nice that Lenny did not know where she lived, so I felt safe at her house.

The trip to Virginia and changing jobs helped, but that did not stop Lenny from all his plans and schemes.

chapter 4

My Insanity

~~~

"The Definition of Insanity is doing the same thing over and over and expecting different results."

Albert Einstein

U nfortunately, Lenny was very persistent. He was an Iron worker working steady and back to working on me to come back to him again. He had been working out of state in New Hampshire on a big job.

I turned eighteen in March, and Jennifer turned three in June. He kept inviting us to come up to New Hampshire to see where he was working and to go to the beach. There were lots of families staying up there in tents. The guys worked the night shift, and the ladies all hung out together with the kids.

Deep down, I still loved him. We started talking more and then seeing each other again when he was in Pittsburgh. Time had passed, and I was starting to think there was hope for us. It seemed like Lenny had matured a bit and changed for the better.

I must admit that our relationship, although volatile, revolved mainly around our sexual chemistry. Part of me knew he was bad for me, but I still could not find the strength and courage to stay away from him. It took me a long time to be able to understand why I had such a hard time getting away from him. I also now know about oxytocin.

Oxytocin is a hormone and neurotransmitter that is involved in childbirth and breastfeeding. It is also associated with empathy, trust, sexual activity, and relationship building. It is sometimes referred to as the "love Hormone" because levels of OXYTOCIN increase during hugging and orgasm. Well, that explains a lot.

Despite all the terrible things Lenny had done to me, I was emotionally bonded with him. I was still in love with the kind, fun and loving Lenny before he became abusive Lenny. I was a sucker for the kind, funny and loving Lenny. The one that showered me with love letters and flowers and made love with me. The one that showed up looking good and wearing my favorite men's cologne, I wish he could just stay that good, kindly guy and never turn to his mean, abusive side.

On one of his trips to Pittsburgh, I met him at our old apartment. The one where we bought the bedroom furniture and decorated together. He still lived there. We made love knowing that we could conceive a child. We were both happy about it when I found out I was pregnant again. The thought of having another child was exciting, like a new beginning. He was Jennifer's father, and I still had hope for us. That was probably part of the deciding factor that Jennifer and I would go to New Hampshire with him for several weeks that summer. I was eighteen and legally old enough to make my own decisions.

Lenny had been on great behavior. He always was when he was trying to get us back. Lenny sent us plane tickets so that Jennifer and I could fly to New Hampshire. He picked us up at the airport, and we went to the beach with the other Iron Worker Families. We stayed in the tent at night when the guys worked. I didn't mind sleeping in a tent until one night we had a bad thunder and lightning storm. The guys had all left for work. Jennifer and I were snuggled in our tent. She had long since fallen asleep.

I was lying beside Jennifer, reading by lantern, and it began to rain, followed by thunder and lightning. The thunder was rumbling so loud that it felt like the earth was rumbling right along with it and lightning was flashing like crazy. We did not have a vehicle to get into because Lenny had taken it to work. I remember laying there praying that we wouldn't get struck by lightning in our tent. It was a very scary night, but the sun came out in the morning, and it was like we never even had a storm.

Things were going well between Lenny and me, and we were excited about building a future together. During the day, after Lenny slept a little, we would go to the beach and play in the sand with Jennifer. We walked around the cute little beach town and went shopping and out to eat.

I had not told my family I was pregnant yet. I guess I was waiting for the right time. As the day was approaching for Lenny to drive Jennifer and me back to Pittsburgh, there was tension between us. Lenny did not want me to be in Pittsburgh while he was working out of town. He wanted me to stay with him, and I needed to get home and take care of some things. He needed to control me, and he could not do that from another state.

The ride home from New Hampshire to Pittsburgh was many long hours, and he was already aggravated that I insisted on getting back home. But he really lost his mind and temper when I started singing along to the radio. I was singing the Daryl Hall and John Oates song "Man Eater." The words are, "oh, oh here she comes, she's a man eater," and he flipped out on me, yelling and swearing, calling me a whore, and a terrible mother and threatening to hurt me over a song! The rest of the ride, my stomach churned, and my mind was racing. What had I done? Jennifer just sat in the back seat, a little child being exposed again to his madness. I could not believe what he was saying and doing. I was afraid I would not make it home alive and was shaking inside. It was like a flip of a switch, and he went from this great guy to a crazed madman. I felt so relieved when we arrived home safely. He was all apologies, but I did not want to hear it. I played it cool and got Jennifer and our bags out of the car.

I woke up the next morning in my bed at home in Pittsburgh crying and realized I was out of my mind. There was absolutely no way that I could have this baby with him. If I was going to survive, if we were going to survive, I could not have this baby. I had no money, and I was no longer on my dad's health insurance. I went to a good friend, that I shall keep anonymous, and asked for her help. She hated the way Lenny treated me, and she did not want me with him. She was also afraid for my safety and Jennifer's safety, so she agreed to help me get the money I needed to pay for an abortion.

This time was different. It was my decision, and I knew I would have to be awake for the procedure. This time I was closer to twelve weeks pregnant. I was terrified but more terrified of Lenny. I went downtown to Planned Parenthood and entered a very large room filled with other women also there to have abortions. I just wanted it to be over. I just remember loud machines and a lot of abdominal pain. Initially, I felt relieved to not be pregnant, but I was in survival mode. My sister Joyce picked me up and took me to her house to take care of Jennifer and me. Joyce and I were always there for each other during difficult periods of our lives without judgement. I just lay in her bed in both physical and emotional pain and cried for hours until I fell asleep. Why did I keep making the same mistakes over and over? Why wouldn't Lenny just leave me alone?

When I talked to Lenny on the phone, I told him I had a miscarriage. I wouldn't see him; I wouldn't talk to him. I wanted nothing to do with him. He was furious. I don't know if he believed me about having a miscarriage or not, I just know he was off the hinges, crazy mad. Thank God he was still working out of State.

I had to go for a checkup several weeks after the procedure. Outside the clinic, there were people praying, and one of them handed me a brochure.

When I got home, I opened the brochure and what I saw was horrifying. Tiny baby parts ripped to pieces in Petri dishes and garbage cans. I wanted to vomit. I curled into a fetal position and sobbed. I wished I had seen those photos before the procedure; I would have changed my mind. I could not believe that as much as I love children, I had done such a horrible thing again. At that moment, I realized how selfish I was and that I had done something horrible, and I wanted to die. I knew that I had to think about my daughter, Jennifer. Who would take care of her if I were not here? I could not let something happen to me and let her go to Lenny.

I was so distraught I thought about somehow luring Lenny into a car and driving off a cliff with both of us in the car so that he would be dead with me and would not get her. I am not sure how I carried on because I wanted to die. I didn't try to kill myself, but years later, my therapist told me I was living suicide. I would put myself in dangerous situations and drink until blacking out when I had someone to watch Jennifer.

I acted like I had it all together for my parents, but I was a mess. I would get babysitters as often as possible, so I could go "out." I just wanted to numb the pain. At the time, I started seeing different older men that usually had plenty of alcohol, cocaine, and marijuana around. Knowing that I was dating other men did not make Lenny go away. If anything, it made him relentless when it came to pursuing me. I did not care what Lenny thought or tried to do to me. I was in my own self-destructive mode.

I had lost many friends because they were all tired of me going back and forth with Lenny. He once hid in the bushes and jumped a guy I was heading out on a date with. When the guy jumped in his car, Lenny started beating up on his car. I jumped on Lenny's back to get him to stop, and my sister Doris broke a chair to Jennifer's little table set over his head. My date drove off, never to speak to me again. My neighbors would see Lenny coming and just yell out for us to call the police. Honestly, I was tired of all of it too.

Lenny was determined that if he could not have me, no one would. I just wanted to be happy, and Lenny kept promising he would be that guy. I was too young and immature to see that he was never going to change. My Dad told me one time, "Sharon, as long as you are with Lenny, you will never know what to expect." My Dad was right.

I was still punishing myself for choosing to have an abortion, and Lenny still thought I had a miscarriage. I was a lost soul at eighteen, trying to raise my sweet daughter, with no self-esteem, no job, and some pretty bad habits.

Lenny had continued working out of State in New Hampshire. That Christmas, he showed up at my house with a full-length, gray rabbit fur coat and, of course, strings attached. There was a diamond engagement ring in the pocket. I didn't want the ring. I didn't want to marry Lenny, but I was like a dust ball blowing in the wind. I wanted the fur coat, so I accepted the engagement ring too. I didn't know what I wanted. I was broken, lost, and confused, and I had no idea what the future held, but once again, I gave Lenny the benefit of the doubt. He knew exactly how to charm me. We spent Christmas week together, and then came New Year's Eve.

We were invited to a party with two of my sisters and their boyfriends. Neither my sisters nor their boyfriends wanted anything to do with Lenny, but they put up with him because they wanted me to go to the New Year's Eve Party.

The party was at the Royal 2. There was food, music, dancing and, of course, Champagne! It was going to be a great time. Early in the evening, Lenny started pressuring me to have Jennifer and I go back to New Hampshire with him. I told him we had just got back together and that we needed to take it slow. I was explaining that we just got engaged and were not married yet, and he was getting madder by the minute.

We didn't even make it to midnight. Our arguing led us outside to his car. At one point, he started choking me, and I shoved my knee into his groin and started running in spiked heels, back towards the Restaurant. Lenny caught up to me, grabbed my long hair, and dragged me back to the car. This was the beginning of another terrifying car ride with Lenny, but this time, I did not have an infant in my arms, and I fought back hard.

After he slammed my head into the dashboard by my hair, I swung around and kicked him in the side of his face with my spiked heel. While my leg was up, he bit me on the back of my leg. It got ugly and by the time the fighting stopped, so did my face. I had two black eyes, two fat lips, bite marks and bruises all over my body.

At first, Lenny would not take me home, but as the sun was coming up, I somehow convinced him that I would not call the police or press charges if he would just take me home. When my family saw me, they were furious, and my dad took me to the Emergency Room to be treated.

Once again, I looked like I had just gone a couple of rounds in a boxing match, but this time so did Lenny. I did not call the police, and I did NOT press charges. I did give Lenny the engagement ring back, but I kept the fur coat. I was not sure if my face would ever go back to the way it was. I and others could not believe that he had bitten me. Slowly the purple bruising and the swelling went away, and the shape of my nose went back to normal. It is amazing how the body heals itself. I wish my spirit would have healed as well as my face.

I knew I needed to do something different if I wanted different results. And I did want different results, not just for me but for Jennifer as well.

chapter 5

With God, All Things are Possible

"It isn't what happened to us that counts, but how we choose to tell the story."

Unknown

I wanted to go back to school and get my life together for Jennifer and me. My lovable little girl kept me going especially when I was feeling down. We were living with my parents, and I went with them to a healing mass. I went to the sacrament of reconciliation because I desperately wanted to start over in a positive way.

Speaking with the priest about everything that had been going on in my life and getting absolution (considered forgiveness from God) helped me feel a little bit better inside and helped me start healing my broken spirit. I felt like God was rooting for me to start taking better care of myself. I knew deep down I was not a bad person, even though I was not happy about some of the choices I had made. I started making plans to go to Community college and get an education, so I could financially support myself and Jennifer.

I applied for financial aid, but they said my father made too much money. I had to find a way to get financial aid so I could enroll in college classes. My friend Joanne whom I worked with at the curtain shop, had recently divorced. We made plans for Jennifer and I, to move in with her and her kids so we could help each other. Living with her, I was able to get the financial aid I needed to go back to school. I had no idea what I wanted to go to school to become, so I just signed up for basic classes. I was also able to get food stamps, and through the WIC Program (Women, Infants and Children), I could get milk, cheese, and other dairy products to help provide more food. My welfare case worker was less than supportive when I told her I was going back to school. She said, "Most girls don't finish." I was determined that one day I would finish and get off the system and be able to support myself and my daughter.

I was busy. To move in with Joanne, I had to patch a hole in the ceiling in the small bedroom that would be my bedroom. After fixing the hole and a little paint and some pretty, white curtains, it was my safe and clean new bedroom. Jennifer was going to share a bedroom with Joanne's daughter Christian. Her son Jason had his own room across the hall. I liked helping her fix up her house. We started working on the kitchen. She had a cool red sink and big wooden cabinets. We picked a wallpaper with strawberries to accent the red sink. One of Joanne's friends hung the wallpaper in the kitchen for us. It felt good adding some personal touches to the kitchen and making it our new home.

I started my classes at our local Community College and was excited even though I had no idea what I wanted to do. I had to start with prerequisite classes and was doing extremely well with my grades even though I still liked to party. I think I mainly kept that to the weekends, so I was able to get by.

Most mornings, I had to wake up early and get Jennifer and me ready for the day. Usually, we would walk to Brookline Boulevard, and I would drop her off at daycare which she really liked. Then I would take two buses to get to school on the north side of Pittsburgh. I would repeat the process in reverse on my way home.

I usually did the cooking of the meals and then would get Jennifer bathed and ready for bed before I even started my homework. Sometimes, my neighbor,

Mario would drive us to school, and we would drop Jennifer off at daycare on the way, which really helped a lot.

I ended the Spring classes of 1983 with a 4.0. To celebrate, I was taking Jennifer to visit my brother Mark and his wife Leanne for a much-needed break in Virginia Beach. We had so much fun swimming in their pool and going to the beach. I was signed up to start fall classes when we got back from the beach.

I decided on medical record terminology for my major, although I'm not quite sure why. I think I picked something in the medical field because I wanted to make a lot of money and be able to find a job. There are lots of hospitals in Pittsburgh. The class was hard and boring. It was basically deciphering doctors handwriting for record terminology or transcription. I never understood why doctors couldn't just write neatly or type so that people could clearly understand what they were saying or prescribing.

I still was not getting any type of child support from Lenny, and we had no visitation schedule set up. Lenny contacted me and asked if I would bring Jennifer and come see his new apartment in Mt. Washington and discuss some type of child support and visitation arrangements since we were not getting back together.

I agreed to meet Lenny to let him see Jennifer and discuss finally getting him to help financially.

We got dropped off at his apartment for our meeting, and all Lenny wanted to talk about was me giving him another chance. He was begging me and explaining how the attic bedroom could be Jennifer's bedroom. I was not interested in hearing any of that, I went to meet him to discuss him helping me financially and to make a plan so he could see Jennifer.

It did not take much, if anything, to set Lenny off and just the fact that I was at the beach and had a nice tan was driving him crazy. I could tell our meeting was not going to be productive in helping me get any child support, so I gave up and decided to leave.

When I started to go get Jennifer from playing upstairs, Lenny lunged at me and grabbed me by the throat. He threw me up against the stairs and shoved his thumb into my windpipe. I could not breathe. I could not get his hands off my throat and knew if I didn't get help, this was it for me. I needed help and fast. The only thing I could think to do was kick the floor as hard and loud as I could to alert the girls living in the apartment downstairs that I needed help.

I thank God that the girls that lived downstairs called the police. It was within a few minutes that police broke down the door and got Lenny off me. They had to pepper spray him to get him in handcuffs. I was not seriously injured other than the huge black and blue handprints on my neck. Jennifer thankfully stayed upstairs and did not witness me nearly being choked to death. She did see Lenny resisting arrest and being handcuffed. The next day she was also telling everyone about us getting a ride home in a police car. I was so angry at myself for thinking I could trust Lenny to have a calm conversation about child support. He lured me there, and when he realized he couldn't control me anymore, he attacked me.

I started back to school for the fall semester, but the old painful memories still haunted me. I still tried to numb the pain with alcohol. I was nineteen years old and had a beautiful four-year-old daughter that I adored, but the two abortions haunted me, and the promiscuity that came with drinking binges did not help my self-esteem at all. I was a mess inside and did not like the person I saw when I looked in the mirror. I was trying to keep it all together, but I wasn't strong enough yet.

One Saturday night in September, I was drowning my sorrows at a party in a bottle of rose' wine. I was drunk, really drunk, and I called Lenny from the party. I was afraid of him, he hurt me many times, but part of me loved him. I also lusted for him. I knew how good he always made me feel in bed. He knew how to please me, and I was clearly not thinking with my brain.

We made plans to meet up, and of course, I went back to his apartment with him. I had drunk sex with him that night and was mortified waking up with him the next morning, head pounding, hung over.

The first thought I had was, "what the hell did you just do?" I did not want to be with him. I basically used him for sex, which I didn't even remember; I was so out of it.

I was right in the middle of my menstrual cycle, and I knew I was way too drunk to think about using birth control. I was not on the pill, and unlike what I was told at fourteen, I was very fertile, just like my mom. My second thought was that I probably managed to mess everything up and get pregnant again!

I also knew that I would rather die than have another abortion. I had absolutely no idea what I was going to do with another baby, but I knew I would figure it out. I waited two weeks to confirm what I already knew.

I will never forget the phone call with my doctor's office. I was on campus at Community College, and I used the pay phone. The nurse confirmed that I was pregnant and then quickly asked me if I was planning to carry the baby or terminate the pregnancy. I was in shock. She was so cold. But the only response that I could mutter was, "I have no idea what I am going to do."

I started to cry, knowing that I would hurt my parents again, knowing I was terrified of Lenny and having no idea how I would be able to handle another child. I did know one thing for sure; I was having this baby. I was the one that was drunk and reckless. It was my responsibility. I made the decisions that led to me being pregnant again. It was time for me to face the consequences of my actions.

As I walked to the bus stop on the corner of the college campus, I was sobbing. I knew that I would not be able to complete the degree program I had started. So many things flooded through my head, and by this point, I was visibly distraught.

There was someone at the bus stop trying to comfort me. I honestly could not tell you if it was a man or a woman. I just know that nothing they could have said or done would have made me feel any better. There was so much pain, shame, and disappointment inside of me, and I felt like such a failure.

That night while lying in my bed at Joanne's house, I prayed the "Our Father" like I had never prayed it before. "Our father who art in heaven hallowed be thy name. Thy kingdom come; thy will be done on earth as it is in heaven. Give us this day our daily bread and forgive us our trespasses as we forgive those who trespass against us and lead us not into temptation but deliver us from evil amen." I reached out to God from my soul, begging for help.

The next morning, I felt a peace inside myself, and the first thought I had was, "call your mother." I so badly did not want to disappoint her again, but I knew that my mother loved me no matter what, and she would help me figure out what to do.

She said there was a Women's Retreat weekend coming up and suggested I go. My response was, "why not." I had absolutely made a huge mess of my life. I had turned against everything I ever believed in and pretty much hated myself. I believed I had nothing to lose and that maybe God could help fix the mess I had made of my life.

A few weeks later, on a Thursday evening in October, I left to attend the Gilmary Retreat Center in Pittsburgh, Pennsylvania.

I felt peaceful from the moment that I arrived. All the women on the team of the retreat knew my parents very well. They also knew that I had a daughter and that I was expecting another baby. There was no judgment from anyone, only love.

The weekend is put on by women, for women. It consists of talks about how their faith and their personal relationship with Jesus Christ affected their lives. For the first time in a long time, I felt hopeful.

The chapel was warm and inviting with candlelight. I knelt before the crucifix hanging above the altar, just crying and crying from the deepest part of my soul. One of the ladies came in and sat with me and told me there was nothing that I could do or that I had done that Christ could not forgive. I felt like they had shown me the love of Jesus Christ as if I had met him in person on that weekend. Somehow, I knew that God was going to help me figure out the right thing to do.

This was a huge turning point in my life because I knew that I was not a bad person but that I had made some bad decisions. I also knew that I was a child of God and that God loved me and wanted good things for me in my life. I thought surely God could fix Lenny to be a good man and a good father. I knew deep down somehow, it was all going to work out. I just didn't know exactly how.

I left the retreat with a sense of hope for the future for Jennifer, myself, and the baby I was carrying. Because of my recommitment to my Catholic Faith, I did not want to just live with Lenny, but we could not get married because I needed the welfare insurance to cover myself and the birth of the baby. I trusted that God was going to make everything right, so I just kept praying about everything and trusting in God.

By the end of October, Jennifer and I moved into the Mount Washington apartment with Lenny. I fixed up the attic bedroom for Jennifer. Half of it was her bed and dresser. The other side was her toy box, her little table and chairs and all her toys.

I fixed up the apartment with a women's touch to make it our little home. Part of my delusion was that if I made everything look nice on the outside, then everything was good. If our apartment looked like a loving family lived there, then that is what we would be. Things had changed quickly, but I was adjusting and was hopeful for the future.

I had quit drinking alcohol, smoking cigarettes, and all recreational drugs while I was pregnant and started taking my prenatal vitamins so the baby would be healthy. Fortunately for me, I am strong-willed, so I was able to do this "cold turkey" because I made up my mind it was best for the baby.

In November, I noticed that I was having some bleeding. I called my doctor's office for advice, and they told me I could be having a miscarriage. They recommended bed rest to see if it would stop the bleeding. It was difficult to get bed rest with a daughter 4 years old, and Lenny was not very helpful, but that is what I did until the bleeding stopped.

One afternoon shortly after I was off the bed rest, I received a very disturbing phone call. The woman on the phone called to confirm my appointment to terminate my pregnancy. I said, "what are you talking about? I never made an appointment to terminate this pregnancy!" I explained that I had just been on bed rest to save this pregnancy. I was so furious that I hung up on her. How dare they assume that just because when I first found out I was pregnant, I said, "I have no idea what I was going to do," that it meant I was not carrying this baby to term. I could not believe she or whomever at that office took the liberty to schedule me for an abortion when that was never my intention. I found that deeply disturbing.

I had no idea how the future was going to work out, but because of my newfound faith, I just knew that somehow everything would work out. I just kept praying and believing.

I would read from the Bible every day and prayed and believed that God was going to work a miracle. God did work miracles, just not like I expected.

Lenny would get so mad when I would spend time reading my Bible like he was jealous of God. He would say to me, "what do you think you're going to be a saint"? I'd say, "I'd like to be."

I was just sixteen weeks pregnant, and I was already showing a little. It was New Year's Eve, and we lived in Mount Washington, one of the highest points in the city of Pittsburgh. The wind was brutal, and it had been so bitter cold that our pipes froze the day before. I was making an appetizer to bring to my sisters Janice's house for her New Year's Eve party. Lenny was recovering from hernia surgery, so he was unable to join us for the evening. Not that he was invited to come anyway. My family disliked him very much and did not want me with him or to have him around. They were constantly worried and prayed for our safety, feeling helpless to convince me on what I should do.

Lenny did not want me to go to my sister's party and was in a mean-spirited mood when he entered the kitchen. He abruptly took the cookie sheet of the spinach ball appetizers that I had prepared and dumped them into the garbage can. Jennifer sat coloring at the dining room table. Somehow, she managed to block out the fighting. Lenny began yelling at me. He loved to insult me and tell me what a bad person and mother I was because he knew that would hurt me the most. I was afraid and confused and had been praying for all that violence to be over so we could have this baby and keep our family together.

I had been praying for a sign from God if Jennifer and I were meant to leave or stay. At this point, Lenny picked up the large knife from the kitchen counter and held it at my pregnant belly, swearing and threatening me. I remember looking into his eyes and, for the first time in my life, realizing that he was no longer the man I had fallen in love with so many years before. His eyes looked dark and scary, like a monster.

I had my answer loud and clear. In fact, I looked up at a plaque that I had on the wall that said, "with God, all things are possible." And I knew that was my sign. It was time for us to go for good this time. I knew that we had to leave and that I would never allow him to lay a hand on me in any way, ever again.

Lenny sat the knife on the kitchen counter and went into the bathroom to get a shower. Without saying a word, I snuck out of the back door of the apartment to go get help while Jennifer continued to color at the table because I knew he would not hurt her.

It was bitter cold, and I didn't have time to grab a coat. I didn't really know anybody on our street, but I walked down the dark street, and I saw a house with large, colorful Christmas lights and a sign that said, "Jesus loves you." I knew that was the house. I went up and rang the doorbell and asked if I could please use their phone. I called my mom, and as soon as she answered the phone, I burst into tears, crying so hard I was hyperventilating. The family whose phone I was using was so kind. They helped me calm down so I could talk and tell them I needed help. My brother Donny was in from New Jersey for the holidays, and he and my dad showed up within fifteen minutes to come to our rescue once again.

When the three of us got back to the apartment, Lenny was gone with Jennifer. He had gone looking for me. My dad started grabbing my stuff and throwing it into large black garbage bags. He said, "we're getting your stuff and we're getting you out of here."

I can't even imagine what I put my family through worrying about our safety 24 hours a day, 7 days a week. I know my family and friends were always in fear for our safety.

When we were packing up the car with what we could grab, Lenny came back with Jennifer. He did not want to hand Jennifer over to me. There was a tense moment between my father, brother Donny, and Lenny. Reluctantly, Lenny handed Jennifer over to me. Thankfully, we avoided another scene involving the police.

Another New Year's Eve messed up by Lenny, but I knew in my heart it was a new beginning for Jennifer and me, without him. I knew that I was finally done getting beat up, both physically and mentally. December 31st, 1983, was the last time that I would allow Lenny to lay a hand on me.

I had finally developed enough self-esteem from my new Christian friends and my strong faith in God to get away from Lenny for good. I had no idea what I was going to do with my future, I just knew it did not include him. I was tired of fleeing into the night with my daughter. I was tired of getting beat up, and I knew that Jennifer and I deserved better.

For the next several weeks after I left the apartment, I tried to make arrangements with Lenny to get the rest of mine and Jennifer's belongings. Every time I set up a moving van, he would not let me into the apartment. After a couple of failed attempts, I decided to take matters into my own hands. I made lists of everything that was mine and Jennifer's, and then I asked Lenny to meet me and go to the doctor's appointment with me about the baby.

He thought we were getting back together. In the meantime, I had arranged for my friends and some family to use my key with my lists and go in and get my belongings while he was with me. They had a good time gathering my belongings, knowing that he was going to be quite furious when he got back.

My doctor's visit went quick, so I took him out to Ponderosa Steak House for our farewell dinner, my treat. As we sat there talking, I knew that he was thinking we were getting back together, and the whole time I was thinking you have no idea what is going on right now. I must admit, it felt pretty good to outsmart him, especially after all the horrible things he had done to me.

When I got back home, our furniture, clothes and Jennifer's toys etc., were spread all over my parents' first floor. I had moved in and out of my parents' home several times, and this time, my father said, "Sharon, if you move out again, you're not coming back." I knew he meant business this time.

But I also know that without my family, I would not have been able to get away from Lenny. They tried so many times to convince me to stay away from him. It wasn't until I finally had enough and I finally had the courage and self-esteem to leave that I could stand up and fight for myself and my future.

Over the next several days, I spent time organizing the bedroom that I once again shared with my daughter Jennifer. We shared a double bed, and somehow, I managed to make room in our bedroom and one closet for all our things. Luckily for Jennifer and me, my youngest brother Neil loved to read to her and play with her. It was great for her and for me.

When researching resources for this book, I found out that one of the first things recommended for someone in an abusive relationship to do is "develop a safe exit plan" for when things get out of control and you know you are ready to be done living with abuse. Have the plan in a safe place with phone numbers to call and know where to go before it is too late. I was fortunate that I had a family to call and a safe place for us to live. The national website provided at the back of this book has a wealth of information, and it is free and confidential.

chapter 6

Adoption is a Loving Option

"When you know better, you do better."

Maya Angelou

A s Jennifer and I settled into a peaceful life living with my family again in my childhood home, my abdomen was growing larger by the day. I had prayerfully made the decision that I was in no financial or emotional position to take on raising another child by myself. I needed to take care of my daughter Jennifer and wanted the baby I was carrying to have a loving family with an emotionally and financially stable environment. I knew I could not provide any of that at that time in my life. I also needed to take care of myself and get some type of education, so I could secure a job and take care of my daughter and myself financially.

Deep down, I knew that it was going to be a difficult decision to live with, but we would both be alive. If I had stayed with Lenny, I believe he would have eventually killed me.

Jennifer and I were alive and well because we had a safe place to go and a support system. I needed another type of help for the child I was carrying.

I contacted an agency called Alternatives to Abortion. It now goes by the name Genesis. I scheduled a meeting with Mrs. Elizabeth Duncan to discuss how to choose a family and go through the process of releasing my child to be adopted by them. I did not know what to expect, but I was open to considering adoption as a possible option.

This was by far one of the hardest decisions that I had ever made in my lifetime, but I knew it was the right thing to do for all of us. When I walked into the room to meet Mrs. Duncan, I expected to see a woman clad in a professional outfit and possibly stern-looking. I was quite happily surprised to see Mrs. Duncan was an older woman with white hair in a bun, a little on the plump side with rosy cheeks and a soft, welcoming smile. She reminded me of the fairy godmother in the animated version of Cinderella.

I instantly loved her. She was the type of woman that cared about helping people in crisis. She took unwed mothers into her home if there was no place for them to go and also helped them keep or release their babies for adoption. This agency had childbirth and childcare classes along with baby clothes and supplies needed for those women keeping their babies. The adoption agency also offered free legal services for women in my situation. The attorney assigned to help me was knowledgeable and assisted me with wise decisions regarding the placement of the baby I was carrying. Another role of the agency was to make sure the home and family I had chosen were suitable for adopting and could properly raise and care for my child.

Mrs. Duncan always went with me to my doctor's appointments. We discussed what I was looking for in a family to raise my child. I wanted parents that were strong in their faith, and that would make sure that he or she would also have a strong faith in God. I wanted her to be raised in a family that had other children because I was so blessed with brothers and sisters. When we discussed this, Mrs. Duncan shared with me that there was a family that came to her mind immediately. She said that the mom had a very bubbly, outgoing personality like mine and that they had adopted a son, so I knew that my baby would have a brother. That meant a lot to me. Mrs. Duncan thought that this family was the right family, and because of my respect for her and the relationship we had formed, I trusted her opinion.

There are different types of adoption, open or closed. Open adoption is where you meet the adoptive parents and stay in touch with them. You can receive cards, letters and photos and even visit with your child in some cases. I knew I could not handle releasing my child and then seeing that child with another family. I felt that would be too heartbreaking every time for all of us and even somewhat confusing for the child. I didn't think I could handle an open adoption plan, but many people prefer that type of relationship.

I still prayed regularly for a miracle, for some way to not have to go through with it, some way to keep my baby. I had to field regular phone calls and harassment from Lenny about getting back together and when the baby was due, but I refused to talk to him.

He would send cards, letters, flowers, friends; any way he could think of to try to get through to me, he utilized it, but it was over, and I knew it. I told him that the baby was not his, in hopes he would leave me alone. One of the things I learned from the adoption agency was that they would have to notify the father to sign papers to release the child. I would not say who the father of my baby was because I knew Lenny would never agree to sign the adoption papers. Not because he loved us, but he loved controlling me.

The attorney handling the adoption informed me that they would have to post the birth of my child in the newspaper with my name for six weeks. I knew it would make me look bad, but I had to do it to protect us. I would not give Lenny any possible way to control the outcome of my future ever again.

It was also suggested that when I gave birth at Magee Women's Hospital that I went in under a different name, so no one would know I was there. The nursery staff was also to put my baby in the back of the nursery for safety.

I started going to a different church on Sundays where people did not know me because I was looking evidently pregnant, and I wanted to avoid unwanted questions. I wasn't due until the end of June, so I stayed in the house a lot because I didn't want everybody to know my business. I did hear rumors that I was selling my baby and other terrible rumors. At first, the rumors hurt me, but then I realized that people are often judgmental when they have no idea what someone else has been through. I learned the hard way that we should never judge a man or woman unless we have walked a mile in their shoes. I learned many lessons on humility throughout this time.

On Mother's Day, 1984, I went to mass at St. Bernard's Church. I was almost eight months pregnant, and they were passing out white roses to all the mothers and expectant mothers at mass. That was the only Mother's Day I got to spend with my baby. That day was very special because the white rose symbolizes purity and life. I know that I made the right choice to choose life for both of us.

Jennifer's fifth birthday was in early June, and we were able to spend a lot of time together because I was not working at the time. I did my best to explain to her that we would not be bringing this baby home from the hospital. I think the most important thing to her at that time was knowing that she was loved and that we were safe. No more seeing her mom with bruises and no more violence.

At the end of June, I was helping my mother by vacuuming in the dining room and realized I was having contractions. I had a doctor's appointment that evening, and Mrs. Duncan was taking me to that appointment. When I got there, the doctor did my exam, and upon realizing that I was in labor, he said, "how far do you live from the hospital?" I said about thirty minutes, and he said, "don't go home, go directly to the hospital." We arrived at about 7:30 PM at Magee Women's Hospital, and my labor progressed quickly. In fact, my mom almost missed it because it went so fast. My sister, Nurse Joyce, was in the delivery room with me. I started pushing at about 9:30, and my healthy baby girl was born at 10:00 PM.

I did not see her that night, but I did want to see her and hold her. Friends of mine that I met through the Women's retreat came to visit and brought me a beautiful 14-karat gold crucifix. They also brought a miraculous medal to pin on her undershirt. There was a beautiful prayer with the miraculous medal that is called the consecration of a child to Mary.

My mom and I were led to a private little room, and a nurse came and placed my baby girl in my arms. My Mom and I prayed the consecration of a child to Mary prayer and pinned the miraculous medal on her little undershirt. I knew she would be safe because the Blessed Mother, Mary, would be watching over her. I held my baby girl in my arms and checked to make sure she had ten fingers and ten toes.

She was beautiful with soft brown peach fuzz hair, blue eyes similar to mine, and her little face just perfect in every way. My Mom held her before we said goodbye, but my father chose not to hold her. I'm sure the entire situation broke his heart because I was his baby girl, and he knew I was hurting, and he wanted so much to protect me. He was a great father, and I did not blame any of this on anyone but myself. I was taking responsibility for my actions in a responsible manner.

Leaving that hospital without my baby girl was heartbreaking, to say the least. It was like leaving a part of my heart outside of my body and believing that it would be taken care of properly. I trusted in Mrs.

Duncan and in the choice that we had made, and I believed in the parents that we had chosen. I knew that once I made this decision, there was no turning back. I could not let another family bond with her and then change my mind and come back in and break their hearts.

I had to be strong. I had to heal from all the trauma I had been through. I had to make plans to get educated and get a job to provide for Jennifer and our future.

When Lenny contacted me to ask when the baby was due, I told him that I had already had my baby and that he didn't have to worry about anything because it was not his. He was furious. He thought he was going to be able to control me again, but it was over. I knew with every cell in my body that it was over, but he was still fighting it.

He threatened to get a lawyer and fight the adoption, and I told him to go ahead and do it. I knew my baby girl was safe, and he would never be able to win.

She would have a wonderful mother and father and the life I wanted her to have, which, under my circumstances, I could not give her. The most important thing to me was that we were all safe and away from Lenny and his unbridled anger and abuse.

It hurt deep in my heart to let her go, but I had faith that someday I would be able to explain it to her in person and that she would understand that it was a matter of survival for all of us.

For more information about adoption, please see the resources at the back of the book.

chapter 7

Summer of 1984 – Worst and Best Summer

~

"We don't develop courage by being happy every day. We develop it by surviving difficult times and challenging adversity."

Barbara DeAngelis

S ummer was in full swing, and I was healing physically and emotionally from giving birth and releasing my child for adoption. I felt sadness, but I also knew I had made the right decision for all of us.

I would take Jennifer to the swimming pool and to Baskin Robins on Brookline Boulevard to get our favorite ice cream.

Not having a car, we walked to and from the swimming pool, so I shed my baby weight fast, and I had a great tan from the days with Jennifer at the pool.

I was twenty years old, and Jennifer had just turned five. While discerning what to do about our future, I made the decision to attend Bradford Business School for Retail Business Management, and classes were to begin in September. I was working on myself and trying my best to move on with my life. My goal was to complete this Business Management course, so I could make enough money to support myself and my daughter.

One day in July, I ran into a Fireman that was a customer of mine when I worked at Anthony's Curtain Shop. I had sold him a Rainbow Bright canopy bedroom set for his daughter's bedroom. It came up that he was no longer married, and he asked me if I would like to go out with him and some of his friends to ride go-karts that weekend and go hear his friend's band play afterward.

I was not interested in dating him, but I hadn't been out with friends or had any real fun for so long that I was excited to go. The evening came, and he picked me up on his motorcycle. We went to a place called Sandcastle and rode go-karts which turned out to be a fun time. Then the group of us went to hear some of their other friends that were in the band playing at a local bar. I had one drink and was dancing and having a good time when I started to feel very strange. I was not drunk; I was drugged! I had not tasted anything in my drink, but it was certainly drugged. Suddenly everything got blurry, and I could not walk by myself. I told Will, not his real name, that I needed to go home.

The next thing I remember was Will, walking me up the steps of his house and into his daughter's bedroom. At this point, I could no longer talk or move. I was aware that he was raping me on his daughter's Rainbow Bright canopy bed. I had sold him this bedding set. My incision from the episiotomy from having my baby was not even all the way healed yet. He knew I just had a baby, and he was raping me. You must be a sick person to do that to another person.

I could not believe he had drugged me and was having intercourse with me against my will. I thought I knew him. I thought we were friends. He roofied me to have sex with me. I didn't know if he used a condom or not; I just knew that it hurt me both physically and emotionally. He did bring me home, but I don't really remember getting there. I kind of remember crawling up the steps to my bed, and that seems to be what happened, but that time is clouded by the drugs I was given. I woke up the next morning in my bed, horrified. All I could think about was, "what if this rapist got me pregnant again?" I felt sick inside and wanted to wash any trace of him from my body. I did not tell anyone what had happened. I think I was equally in shock and denial. Later that day, the rapist called me and tried to act like we had sex, consensually. I told him he was out of his mind and to never, ever come near me or call me ever again. My coping mechanism at that time was to act like it did not happen. I had sex before, so I just tried to act like it was no big deal. Just forget about it and move on. I prayed every day that I would get my next period, and I cried tears of joy and relief when I finally did get my period. I don't think I would have been able to get through this difficult time in my life If I did not have my faith in God. I believed deep down that; somehow, I was going to get through this.

I was still emotionally dealing with the heartbreak of releasing my baby girl for adoption. I certainly could not deal with being date raped. If I did not talk about the date rape or tell anyone about it, I could pretend it never happened. Unfortunately, I would still see the date rape Fireman sometimes because he was at the Firehouse on the corner on Brookline Boulevard right by where I lived, but I acted like I did not know him or see him. I stuffed down all my feelings about the date rape. It would be years before I allowed myself to process what happened to me that night.

I wish I had reported what happened and had him arrested for raping me. I wish I had gone to the hospital and had a rape kit done. I simply was not strong enough at that time. I write about it now because words have power, and maybe sharing this story will give someone else the courage to speak up for themselves and get help.

I cannot go back and change the way I responded to my rape, but I can shed light and hope for others. All rapes are not the same. It could be a stranger and violent or even a family member. Rape is still rape, and it's never okay, no matter who the perpetrator is. No one has the right to force sexual intercourse or any unwanted sexual acts upon you.

I put on my brave face, my mask of "I am okay," and marched on because I am a survivor, and that was all I could do to keep going at the time. By August, I was moving on with my life and being courageous, not just for me but for Jennifer. I needed a car, and I wanted to be able to afford a nice apartment and raise my daughter. I told my mother that I hated men and that they were only interested in one thing. I didn't need or want a man in my life. Men had only hurt me, and I would not let them win.

My mother told me her grandmother had always told her to pray for a good man in her life. My mother certainly did get a great man in my father. So, one day I said to God something like, "Okay, God, you know my life. If there is a man that can handle my life – bring him." That was my prayer at the beginning of August, and I wasn't really expecting to get an answer any time soon.

Jennifer and I went with my family to the beach in Belmar, New Jersey, to visit my oldest brother, Donny and his wife. We stayed with her family at their beach house. It was nice to get out of Pittsburgh and have some fun at the beach. It was so nice for Jennifer because she and my brother Neil got to play together. We built sand sculptures, rode the waves, went to the boardwalk, and she got to ride the rides at the amusement park. It was so nice to know we were safe and Lenny was out of the picture.

Two weeks after my prayer about finding a good man, my friend, Kathi, was bugging me to go with her to her boyfriend Tom's work picnic. I was not interested in going, but she kept insisting that it would be fun and that I should go with her. I finally gave in to her repeated requests. When Kathi came to pick me up, I hopped in the back seat and was surprised to see Tom's brother John who had been picked up before me. I had met John before, but I was engaged to Lenny, and he was dating a girl I knew from High School. John was handsome with dark brown hair and dark brown eyes with a kind smile. He also had a black eye and a splint on one of his fingers. I was so curious as to what had happened to him. On the ride to South Park for the picnic, he told me the story of helping his friend, a manager at the famous Primanti Brothers, make fries and getting his hand smashed, then passing out and hitting his face on the stainless steel sink, and getting the black eye. The ride to the picnic went fast because we talked the whole time and just hit it off.

At the picnic we played volleyball, softball, caught frisbees and had lots of good food. When it got dark outside, someone started playing the guitar, and we were all singing along. John and I had a great time together. John was such a gentleman and offered to walk me to the bathroom with a flashlight. He knew I had a daughter, and he even knew of Lenny and how crazy he was known to be. Despite all that, while we were walking by flashlight, John asked me if I would be interested in going out on a date with him sometime.

I was shocked that he asked me out and that I felt excited about it. There was something special about John. I told him I would really like it if we could go out sometime. We rode home in the back of his silver van, sitting in a tire. Because John's brother Tom had put the picnic together, he had driven the van with a grill and other stuff. When we arrived at my house, I gave John a quick kiss to let him know I was looking forward to seeing him again.

John called me later in the week to make plans for our first official date. He asked what I was doing Friday evening, and I told him my daughter, Jennifer, had a dentist appointment and fully expected him to pick another night. Instead, John asked if we needed a ride to the dentist's office. I was surprised but accepted the offer since I did not have a car and we had to take two buses each way.

On our first date, John showed up in his clean, silver work van with a lawn chair in the middle for Jennifer to sit in. We drove to the dentist appointment, and John and I sat and talked while Jennifer saw the dentist and got her filling. After the dentist appointment, my mom babysat Jennifer, so John and I could go out for a little while.

I asked what he was doing on Saturday, and he told me he was going to be painting his apartment. He had purchased a 4-unit building to use one unit for his Heating and Cooling business office and sheet metal shop, two apartments to rent out, and one apartment for him. He was working on his apartment when we met. I offered to help him paint his apartment, and he was happy to have the help.

The next day John and I painted several rooms in his apartment. I think John was surprised to find out that not only did I like to paint, but I was also very good at it. I always liked to decorate and make things look nice, especially since I had worked at the curtain shop. We finished up painting and headed to a local favorite pizza place called Fiories. I finished my half of the calzone and the rest of his ½ that he could not eat. We had worked hard, and I had worked up quite an appetite.

I really liked John, and I could tell he liked me too. One of the most important things to me was that Jennifer really liked John too. However, I did not want my relationship with John to go any further until we really talked. The next time John asked me out, I told him that I needed to tell him a few things about me before we went any further. I needed to make sure he understood who I was, what was important to me and what he was getting himself into.

We went to a little Mexican Restaurant and got some food and sat and talked. I told John that Jennifer and I were a package deal. I was not interested in dating someone that did not understand that my daughter was a huge part of my life. If he wanted to be with me, it meant being with us. I also wanted John to understand that he could be in danger because Lenny was still harassing me. I told John some of the stories of other guys I tried to date and how Lenny would hide in the bushes and how he attacked my one date, and how Lenny started kicking and punching his car. I also did not want John to hear about my releasing a baby for adoption from someone else. It is a small town, and I wanted him to hear it from me.

John asked me how many years ago I had released my baby girl for adoption and was surprised to find out that it had only been two months because I had lost all the weight. John said he had a lot of respect for me for going through the entire pregnancy and releasing that child to a family that could not have children. He knew from how much I loved Jennifer that releasing my baby girl had to be a really hard thing for me to do. He also said he knew I had a daughter when he asked me out. Then John said, "Lenny is not going to scare me away." My response was, "well, you have been warned."

John had a very calm personality and was nothing like Lenny, so I truly felt he had the right temperament to not let Lenny get to him. John would say and do the nicest things. Like if I was stressed out about something, he would say, "What is the worst thing that can happen? If you can handle that, then everything will be okay." He was so calm, and I loved that about him.

The following Sunday, I invited John to join our family for our Church Picnic. It started with mass, and then there were water balloon tosses, other games and prizes and tons of great food and desserts. There was a great playground for the kids, and Jennifer was having a blast.

John and I had only been seeing each other for two weeks, but I already had developed strong feelings for him. The picnic grounds were covered with beautiful trees and flowers, so John and I decided to go for a walk alone. While walking, we stopped and leaned up against a tree, and John asked me if it was okay if he fell in love with me. I was so happy to hear him say that because I was already falling in love with him. The way he was with me, the way he treated Jennifer, and my family really loved him. John was kind, respectful and hardworking and from a really great family. We shared similar values as well, and all of that meant the world to me.

June and July of 1984 had been two of the worst months of my life, even though I had plenty of other terrible experiences, but in August, things started looking hopeful again. I had met John, such a loving and special man, and I knew within a short time that he was the man I was going to marry someday. I was starting Bradford Business School soon, and I was beginning to see my determination for a better life pay off. I was not going to let all the prior pain and heartache tear me apart. One of my favorite poems is the Footprints poem. Many people are familiar with this poem. It talks about going through difficult times in our lives and that the Lord Jesus promises to be there with us, especially at our lowest points in life. Then the writer says, "Lord, I noticed that at the saddest and lowest times when I needed you the most, there was only one set of footprints in the sand. Why would you leave me when I needed you the most?" And the Lord replies, "I love you and would never leave you. When you see only one set of footprints in the sand, it was then that I carried you." Trust me when I tell you, there were many, many times I felt that the Lord carried me when I surely did not feel I could have or would have made it on my own. It was then that He carried me!

RESOURCES FOR RAPE VICTIMS ARE ON THE RESOURCES PAGE AT THE BACK OF THIS BOOK

chapter 8

Determination for The Life I Wanted

~

"The most difficult thing is the decision to act.

The rest is merely tenacity."

Amelia Earhart

I was loving my classes at Bradford Business School; Jennifer was in Kindergarten and John was busy running his HVAC Company. John's mother, Lorraine, helped him run his business in the office with the books and answering the phones, but John and a helper did the install work. John also went out on the service calls himself which meant that sometimes if I wanted to see him, I had to go on NO HEAT calls with him at night. I didn't mind because we just loved being together.

John fell in love with my large, loud family and Jennifer and I were very loved and welcomed by John's family. The first Thanksgiving we were dating, Jennifer and I were invited for dinner at the Wahl's house.

We were all sitting around the table and Jennifer said, "I can't wait to hear," and she started singing, "here comes the bride, all dressed in white!" I wanted to sink under the table but the whole family burst into laughter at her sweet sentiment. As the saying goes, "out of the mouths of babes." Christmas of 1984 was one of the best I ever had and by New Year's Eve, I was sure this was the real deal.

The Business Course I was taking at Bradford Business School was ten months long and I was learning a lot. I had to work an internship as part of it and I had lots of homework, but I loved challenging myself. One of the classes was Psychology, and I had to read the book "I'M OK – YOU'RE OK." This class helped me so much to understand why Lenny did some of the things he had done, like throw beer in my face or try to control me.

The instructor helped me to stop letting Lenny control and upset me with his phone calls. There was no such thing as caller ID, so you had to answer the phone to see who was there.

My instructor told me that as soon as I answered the phone and heard Lenny's voice, I was to hang up the phone and not listen to his words. "Don't listen to anything he says and don't say anything, just hang up," he urged me to be strong and stand up to my abuser. He said if Lenny wanted to see Jennifer, he could file for visitation with the Courts in Family Division. So that's what I did. No more listening to mean things and no more tears. I was not giving him any opportunity to upset me. I was taking control.

In June of 1985, I graduated with a 4.0 – High Honors and shortly after that got a good job at Joseph A. Bank Clothiers. I was making money now, supporting Jennifer and myself. I gave my parent's money for food and rent. I was so proud of myself for finally proving to my Welfare Case Worker that I would finish school. I was a bit sidetracked, but I did not give up and I did finish, with honors. I did not do it alone though. I did have the support of my family, friends, and John. I could not have done it alone, especially without my mom volunteering to take care of Jennifer when she got home from school until I got back in the evenings. She was always supportive. We all need support along the way, after all.

I wanted to get some financial support from Lenny since his iron-worker job paid him way more money an hour than I made, so I went to Family Court and filed for child support. Up until this point, I had never received any child support from Lenny. I also let him know that he was free to file for visitation but that he could no longer contact me directly.

The day of the child support hearing arrived, and Lenny did not show up in court. Because I knew he was iron working and making a lot of money, the Judge ruled in my favor and planned on having his wages attached. The problem with getting his wages attached was iron workers move around from one job to the next. Back then it was hard to get the money even though I won in court.

I had also heard from a reliable source that Lenny had been arrested in January for possession of cocaine with the intent to deliver and there was absolutely no way I was letting him take my daughter and be dealing drugs.

I let Lenny know that if he filed for visitation, I would request supervised visitation.

Lenny was losing his mind. He was court-ordered to pay child support, I would not speak to him, and he was not seeing Jennifer. And by now, he knew I was in a serious relationship with John.

One Saturday afternoon, John and I were in his sheet metal shop and to our surprise, Lenny came walking in the double side doors. He was venting about not seeing Jennifer and trying to scare me into not requesting supervised visitation. Lenny put his hand on a metal pipe that was sitting on a work bench and looked straight at John and threatened to blow his head off.

We stayed calm. Lenny turned around and left the shop assuming he had accomplished scaring us into submission. However, as soon as Lenny left the shop, I called the police, and we reported the terroristic threats that were made.

Within a couple weeks, we were all before the local Magistrate, Charlie McLaughlin. He had seen me in there before with Lenny years earlier when he kicked my Parent's front door off the hinges. The Magistrate told Lenny that he better quit bothering us, and that if anything happened to us, even if he didn't do it, constables would be coming to arrest him. It was really good that we filed this police report because it would end up helping us in the future.

When we finally went to court at the Family Division, Lenny was awarded supervised visitation at the home of my sister Joyce every Saturday from 1:00 to 3:00 PM until further review. I was at work, so I never had to see him. I believe he came three times and then he stopped coming. I never did get any child support, but the arrears were building up.

John and I had been dating for fourteen months then and we were so happy. We had plans to go to the October Fest in town, but John was acting different than usual when he picked me up. Instead of heading into town, he made a turn and headed up to Grandview Avenue to the best views of our city.

We walked over to one of the scenic pads. To my surprise, he got down on one knee and pulled out a beautiful Marque diamond engagement ring set in yellow gold. John told me that he had my father's blessing and would be honored if I would be his wife. He was smiling from ear to ear. Even when I said yes and kissed John, he was still smiling. It was one of the happiest moments of my life and one that at many times I thought would never happen for me.

I could not wait to tell our family and friends that John and I were engaged. Many of them already knew that he was planning on proposing. My engagement ring was beautiful and I was on cloud nine. We were so excited about getting married! We didn't want a long engagement but there was no way to have a small wedding with such a huge family. We needed some time to plan, and I wanted to save some money to help my parents with the cost of the wedding.

I felt like I was in a wonderful dream. John and I were getting married, and we were going to be a happy family. Despite all the terrible things I had been through, I was in love with a wonderful man, and we were getting married. Life was good!

Right after we got engaged, John showed me a duplex he wanted to buy and renovate. I knew his dream was to own more rental property. This duplex had been vacant for two years and the bank that owned it did not want the place. It was a dump. It needed new windows, a new roof, two full Kitchens, carpet, plaster and paint, and new garage doors - basically it needed everything. But he bought it, and we started working on it every minute we could when we were not at work.

John's parents came to help, and we even had Jennifer knocking old tiles off in the bathrooms. It was a lot of work, but John's mom would bring food and drinks and we would make a day of renovating until we dropped. Lorraine and I tore out the old carpet and had to scrub the walls before we could even paint them. John and his dad, Bill, got their hands dirty in the duct work for the new forced air heating and cooling system, and built bulk heads to cover the new duct work.

We had a company put in the windows and a new roof. We worked for months but we got it looking really good. John showed me the ropes on how to find good tenants. This was a new role for me as a landlord, but it was something I would be doing from then on.

I always liked interior decorating and fixing things, so this was a good fit for me. John and I liked doing this together and we liked that it helped us out financially.

When we were not working on the Duplex, we were planning our wedding. We set the wedding date for July 5th, 1986. That gave us nine months to plan for our big day. Father Dan DiNardo, now Cardinal DiNardo was a very special priest in my life and had helped me many times in my life. He was in Rome at the time so I wrote to him to let him know I was engaged to marry a wonderful man and wanted to find out if he would be back in Pittsburgh to possibly marry us. He wrote back letting me know he would still be in Rome in July and unable to marry John and I, but he was overjoyed that I had met such a wonderful man. He did give me a lot of credit for "my sheer determination for a better life." I really want to find that letter because his words meant so much to me.

Since Father Dan, as we called him was not able to marry us, we decided to get married at John's family church, St. Catherine of Sienna and follow up with the reception for three hundred people at St. Pamphilus Church Hall.

We decided on a semi-sit down for our reception dinner and a D.J. for the music so we could pick the songs we liked. We hired a florist, photographer and John's Uncle Paul agreed to video record the wedding for us. We picked a baker to make a multi-tiered cake with lights, waterfalls, flowers and the traditional bride and groom on top of the cake.

In Pittsburgh, there is the tradition of having a cookie table. We had people baking dozens of every kind of cookie you could imagine.

We had decided on a resort in Captiva Island off the Florida coast for our Honeymoon. We picked a restaurant with a beautiful garden and water fountain for our rehearsal dinner, so we could be outside for some nice pictures.

My five bride maids and I picked peach colored, tea length dresses with cute little hats to match. It was the 80's, that' all I can say about that. My then sister-in-law, Linda, asked me if I would be interested in borrowing the wedding dress that had been hand made for her in Italy by her aunt. I remembered how gorgeous it was and of course, I said yes to that. The chest had sheer white material with rows of different types of tiny beads in a V shape. The sleeves were the same sheer white with a small white ruffle at the wrists. It accentuated my tiny waist and had a full skirt bottom with embroidered roses below the waist. I felt like a princess in that dress. I had to have alterations to make it fit me, but it saved me a small fortune. I picked out my head piece with beads and roses to match the dress and classic white satin pumps.

The months flew as we planned the wedding. We picked out beautiful wedding invitations and June was approaching so it was time to get them in the mail. One of the hardest parts of the entire process was making the seating arrangement for the reception. Who was going to sit with whom and at what table?

Jennifer was just finishing first grade and she was about to celebrate her birthday right before my bridal shower. It way an extra special birthday because Jennifer loves dogs. John was surprising her with a dog. Chris was a rescue dog from a family that could not keep him. He was a Siberian Husky with beautiful blue eyes. He was big, but she loved him. Chris would live at John's until we got married and we moved in to the apartment. It was a beautiful hot day and after the party, we decided to hop in John's pickup truck and take some of the kids to Dormont swimming pool. The day could not have been any better. It was probably one of Jennifer's best birthdays ever.

Sunday, June 8th was my bridal shower put on by my mom and Johns' mom, my four older sisters and my friend, Kathi, who was now engaged to John's brother, Tom. My sisters and Kathi were all bride's maids. The shower was a brunch with many kinds of homemade quiches, fresh fruit, pastries, and a huge sheet cake. There must have been eighty women there, family, friends, and coworkers. I felt like I opened gifts for hours. John had some dishes and cookware in his apartment, but we got so many nice things that we really needed. It was so nice to have such beautiful new things to start our married life with.

John showed up at the shower to help pack up and transport all our gifts to his apartment. We felt closer to each other now and were so excited that the wedding was only twenty-seven days away. John had started making room in his closets for my clothes and we built a bedroom for Jennifer by closing off part of the huge open space that was a living room-dining room combination.

It was so nice to be loved by such a kind, loving and gentle man. John and I did not fight even if we disagreed. He would never even swear at me let alone hurt me physically. He was physically strong and muscular but extremely patient and thoughtful. Johns' personality was the opposite of what I had experienced with Lenny.

As our bridal shower came to an end, I felt like I was in a beautiful dream. My real prince had rescued me and Jennifer from the terrible bad guy. And now we were going to ride off into the sunset together. We had planned our beautiful wedding and a fairytale honeymoon, and we were ready to start our new life together.

chapter 9

Shattered; Miracle Needed!

~

"Faith is the strength by which a shattered world shall emerge into the light."

Helen keller

On Monday morning, June 9th, I was getting ready for work and in a great mood because of having an amazing weekend. But I could not ignore this nagging feeling in my gut. I had to take the bus into town for work. I got on the bus right by my house with a neighbor, Rosemary, that I was friends with growing up. She had been at my shower the day before. I started to tell her that John and I had agreed on him taking a guy trip to visit a friend of his, Scott, that was living in Ocean City, Maryland. It was important to me that he knew that I trusted him.

The problem with this trip was John and the other guys were all going on their motorcycles. John had a shiny white Honda Interceptor with red and blue stripes. It was a very fast bike and could go from 0 to 100 miles per hour in a matter of seconds. I knew he was going to wear his leather clothes and helmet, but I just had a bad feeling about it being too close to the wedding. I later found out that my dad also had bad feelings about this trip.

When I got to work, everyone was excited to talk about the shower and how nice everything was. I got busy and the day was flying by. My shift that day was twelve hours, 9 am to 9 pm so around 5 pm, I punched out for my dinner break. Before I got to sit down, I heard on the intercom that there was a phone call for me.

When I picked up the phone, it was John's oldest brother Billy. He said, "John's been in an accident." It sounded like he was laughing hysterically, which I thought was a terrible thing to joke about, but then I realized, he was crying hysterically. He said, "all we know is that it is bad, your mother is packing you a bag, we are coming to get you." John's friend Scott was on the back of the motorcycle when they crashed. He was burnt and cut up but was able to call right away to tell us to get there. I stood there in shock for I don't know how many minutes before going to find my manager Lori to tell her I had to leave.

When I found Lori standing with her mom, I could not get the words out of my mouth. I stood there shaking and I just started to cry. Somehow, I managed to tell them what was happening. Lori's mom took hold of my arms and looked me in the eyes. She said, "you have to be strong now, not just for John but for his mom, you have to be strong." I felt anything but strong. I felt physically ill, terrified, worried but not strong. I quickly managed to gather my things and go. My dad picked me up and took me to say goodbye to Jennifer and to grab my suitcase.

We had no idea what to expect. Did he lose a limb, was he paralyzed? We had no information.

The next thing I knew, my dad was speeding down the highway to get John's parents, Bill & Lorraine, and I to the airport. The flight was at 7 PM. We arrived at the airport with so little time that we could not check our bags. They were holding the plane for us. We were running through the airport with our suitcases. I thought John's father, Bill was going to have a heart attack. When we finally boarded the plane, we sat red faced and speechless. We were all terrified. Was John still alive? Were they waiting till we got there to give us the awful news. We had no idea what to expect, only that it was not good. The entire evening was torture, not knowing.

We landed from our first flight and boarded a tiny sixteen passenger airplane to get us closer to where John was taken. It was not a pleasant flight, especially since it was such a tiny plane. We landed a second time and entered a small airport that was reporting about the motorcycle accident, it was on the news. John had crashed into a restaurant that thankfully was closed at the time of the accident. It was shocking to see it on TV. I was still in shock and hoping I would wake up and this would all be a terrible nightmare.

John's uncle, Sam, and his wife, Eva, met us at the airport and drove us to the hospital where they had taken John. When we arrived at the first medical facility, we found out that his injuries were too severe, and he was taken by ambulance several hours away to The Baltimore University Shock Trauma Unit. They wanted to life-flight John, but he had a head trauma, and they could not sedate him.

That's when we found out John was not wearing his helmet when he crashed. He always wore his helmet. It was the state law in Pennsylvania, and he always wore it. In Maryland, a helmet was not required.

Thank God for Sam and Eva. They drove us on that black, moonless night to Baltimore University

Hospital. We arrived after midnight. The last several hours seemed like an eternity. We were met by doctors and nurses that tried to prepare us on what to expect.

When John lost control of the motorcycle, he went up over a curb onto a sidewalk and into a brick wall, the entranceway to the restaurant. The right side of Johns face and upper body took most of the trauma. He had crushed his right cheek bone, broke the eye socket, and bruised the front of his brain. There were three quarter sized bruised on the front of John's brain in the areas that control personality, judgement and memory. The right side of his face and ear was one huge purple bruise. The swelling was massive.

There were several cuts and lacerations on his shoulder and arm but those were minor compared to the head trauma. We were instructed to put on what looked like blue shower caps and blue garments to cover our street clothes. The doctors told us that Johns short term memory was affected and that he might not recognize us. Since I knew him less than two years, they said he might not recognize me. They said we might have to date all over again. This could not be happening. Don't they know we are getting married in twenty-five days? I found myself questioning silently as tears stained my face. I could not believe this was happening. I think I was in shock because I just remember going through the motions but not being able to comprehend reality.

When John saw the three of us standing near his bed, he reached out for his mother. He knew who she was. When John saw his dad, he thought his dad was a woman, named Marcell, that was dating one of their relatives.

John did not know who I was. I was crushed. Just a day before, I was on cloud nine and now everything was crashing down around me, around us. It felt like I was in a beautiful bubble filled with love and in a split second, the bubble burst and hope for our future was shattered.

We were told that once John was stable and the swelling went down a little, we could discuss how to go about repairing the broken bones in his face. We went to our hotel to get some rest, so we could try to deal with what would come next.

I called my mom to try to tell her what was happening, but I could not speak. I just sobbed, and she listened. My mom told me that she and my dad had put John on our Church Prayer Chain. She told me how many people were praying and fasting for us. That meant a lot to us because we really needed a miracle. The Doctors could not give us any guarantees so the more prayers, the better.

Tuesday, June 10th, we arrived at the hospital to begin meeting with more doctors, specialists in facial reconstruction, brain specialists, and social workers. The plan to repair John's face was to take a curved piece of his rib to be used to recreate the eye socket and to use stainless steel to replace his crushed cheek bone. They would make a small incision under his lower eye lashes and slide the new stainless cheek into place. We had to sign so many papers saying we understood all the risks of just about everything and anything that could go wrong but we had to do the surgery. We also felt confident in the surgeon because we were at one of the best hospitals in the country, maybe in the world.

The head injury was another story. The staff was aware that our wedding day was quickly approaching, and they were recommending that we start the process of canceling the wedding.

My head was spinning, and I was starting to realize how severe his brain injury was.

The facial reconstruction surgery was done on Wednesday, June 11th, and thankfully it went well. John was out of it the rest of the day, so we really did not get to see him awake again until Thursday, June 12th.

When we saw John awake for the first time, the doctors asked him if he knew who I was. He had a hard time talking because of the drainage tube up his nose and the surgery on his face but he managed to say my name, Sharon Graham. They asked, "who is she"? and John said, "my wife." He was confused but he knew my name. He thought we were already married. When we told him that we were thinking of postponing the wedding until he was better, he said "no, I'll be there."

The problem was not John being there physically. His cuts and bruises would heal, his bones would heal but the doctors could not tell us what would happen with his brain. Every person's recovery is different. John was at times very childlike, he was not the same person I fell in love with, and I was not sure if he remembered the past twenty-two months that we had been dating, the things we had done and our hopes and plans for our future. He did not remember getting Jennifer the dog Chris for her birthday or anything from the bridal shower or that weekend. Thankfully, he did not remember the accident.

The doctors told us to wake John up when we were with him and talk to him to bring him back to reality. I had photos in my wallet, and we would hold them up and ask him who they were. We started getting cards and letters from family and friends that were praying for us. We got plants, fruit baskets, and flowers. It was helpful knowing so many people cared. We hung the cards and letters on the wall and before long, it was covered.

It was difficult being in the shock trauma unit because everyone there was in such bad shape. They were literally putting people back together. I could not stand the smell of the place. One day I think it all hit me like a ton of bricks. I still did not know if my fiancé was ever going to be well again. I did not know if the man I loved was ever going to be my husband. What was I going to do about the wedding that was now in twenty days? I had already been through so much in my life before I met John and I was finally happy, we were happy. How could this be happening? I remember walking out of the hospital and just walking with tears streaming down my face. I came upon some type of church, and I sat down on the steps. In my heart I had a conversation with God from deep in my soul. God knew the hell that I had been through before I met John and He knew my heart was broken again. I pleaded with God to fix John. I let God know that we all needed John to have a complete recovery.

I truly did not think I could put the pieces of Sharon back together again. I had done it too many times already and I was only twenty-two years old. He had to come back to me, to us.

After the first week of living in a hotel and eating all our meals out, John's Dad, Bill, had to head back to Pittsburgh to run his Barber Shop and help with John's heating and cooling business. Lorraine and I stayed with John since we could not move him yet. At the end of the second week after the accident, we were able to make plans to transport John by ambulance to a rehabilitation hospital back in Pittsburgh. It was great to be going home, to be surrounded by family and friends, especially during this scary time with no idea what the future was going to look like.

Some people with the type of head trauma as John would have seizers and/or severe headaches for the rest of their lives. Some people can't remember how to get home when they leave the house or have other memory issues. There were many things we did not know about the future but one decision we had to make was what to do about the wedding and the honeymoon. It was now June 25th and our wedding was just ten days away.

With the help of my parents and John's parents, we made the decision to wait to see how John would recover and what he would remember before we would get married.

Since there was no such thing as email and this is before cell phones and texting, my family helped me with the arduous task of canceling the wedding we had planned for nine months. It was Saturday, June 29th, one week before the wedding. The dreaded day of making phone calls to cancel our dream wedding had come.

My mom and sisters along with John's mom and other family, started calling all the guests to let them know that John and I would not be getting married on Saturday, July 5th. I had the job of calling the church, the Reception Hall, the caterer, the DJ, the florist, photographer, the restaurant for our rehearsal dinner and canceling our flights and hotel for our honeymoon at Captiva Island. To tell the accident story over and over was emotionally draining.

By the end of the day, It was done and the wedding was officially canceled. Everyone was kind to me and felt terrible about the situation. It was a miracle that we did not lose any money. No one charged us for cancelling the wedding with only one-week notice. Everyone said that when John was well again, they would be delighted to help us have our wedding. I needed my groom to get well before I could think about planning it all over again.

I am not sure how I managed to go back to work but I had to. I went through the motions of life, but I was not okay. John was still in the hospital and was slowly making improvements.

Some days he would seem fine and other days he would see birds flying in his room or say bizarre things, like threaten to throw his pizza at me for trying to get him to eat. He lost about twenty pounds from having a feeding tube up his nose, so we would encourage him to eat to put some weight back on.

On July 4th, the day before we were supposed to get married, John was released from the hospital. I was at home folding some laundry and John showed up at my house. I could not believe that he was there. What was also more strange was the fact that no one else was home.

This was the first time we had seen each other out of a hospital since June 8th, the day of my bridal shower, the last time we were so happy, putting all our gifts in what was going to be our new home. It just felt so good to kiss him and be in wrapped in his arms and not in a hospital room. We laid on my bed, holding each other. Our wedding was supposed to be the next day but for now, it was canceled. We did not know what the future held but we were hopeful. Up to this point, the doctors were amazed at how good he was recovering but they gave us no guarantees for complete recovery. John's surgeons did an amazing job on his face reconstruction and he looked as handsome as ever, just a lot thinner. We even managed to save his mustache.

Saturday, July 5th, was going to be a difficult day to get through. We were supposed to be getting married at 5:00. The sun was shining, and the sky was clear and blue not a single cloud in sight. But instead of getting married, John and I headed to the Marriott Swimming pool with his parents and some of their friends.

All day I kept thinking this is when I was supposed to get my hair done, and now we would be getting to the church. I just laid there with my eyes closed with tears of sadness running down my checks. I could not pretend like I was fine. My heart hurt because I did not know if the man I was in love with, would ever be my husband. John was getting better but as I said before, with head injuries everyone's recovery is different.

We had to start dating again. John continued to go to rehabilitation for his brain injury, so they could test his math and writing skills along with memory and recognition. I would ask him all the time about things we had done to see what he remembered. John and his friends had taught me to snow ski, so I asked him things about our ski trips and things like that to see what he could recall.

While John was making progress, I was suffering inside. This ordeal had taken a huge tool on me. I was doing my best to hold myself together, but my mom could tell I was struggling.

None of us knew what the future was to hold but my mother knew that the past was making this current situation more difficult to endure. She too was hoping and praying John would make a full recovery, not just for him but for me and Jennifer.

This accident was affecting all of us. We were all ready to be a family and it felt like it was ripped away from us. John had been the father to Jennifer that she had not had, and now we needed him to recover. He has been like our knight in shining armor riding in on his white horse to save us. John rode in a silver Chevy van, not on a horse, but he did show up to rescue us from the evil villain.

One day at a time through the month of July and into August, I managed to go on. I got up and went to work. John was getting a little better every day. He had to go back to work because it was his company. His employee, Tim, had managed to keep some things going while John was in the hospital. Lorraine was back to taking care of the answering the company phone, scheduling customer appointments, and taking care of paying the bills.

John was passing the physical and cognitive tests they were giving him in the outpatient program. We spent as much time together as we could and by the middle of August, just two months after John's life-threatening motorcycle accident, with a brain injury, we decided that he was well enough to start planning our wedding again. Hallelujah!

I was happy but a little nervous. We could not get the Reception Hall for our wedding on a Saturday for a really, long time, so we decided to get married on Friday, October 10th, 1986. We had to change a few other things as well. It was not good to go to Captiva Island in October because of hurricane season. Two of my customers at Jos. A. Bank Clothiers were travel agents and they highly recommended Sandals in Montego Bay, Jamaica. Sandals is an, all inclusive, resort for adults only. They raved about this place. Initially, we thought it was too expensive, but they were able to get us a really good price, so we booked Sandals for our one week honeymoon. The original cake lady was not available for October 10th, so we had to find another baker. It is funny that what seemed really important before John's accident did not matter as much anymore. What did matter was we were both alive and well. Things like the cake, seating arrangement and other things seemed quite trivial.

John was doing even better than the doctors predicted and was back to work in July when they had thought he wouldn't be able to go back for months, with no headaches and no seizures. He was a walking miracle!

The only important thing to me was that John had survived his motorcycle accident and was making a miraculous recovery both physically and mentally and we were getting married.

After we rescheduled the wedding, my mom had shared with me that John's accident was one of the saddest times in her life. She knew that after everything I had already been through that if John did not recover, and we were not able to get married, I would have been devastated. She was right. I felt like my belief in happiness would have been shattered. But love and faith won. John fought to get his health back to where he was before the accident so we could get married.

In the months surrounding John's motorcycle accident, surgery, and recovery, I felt like I was in a nightmare of hell. I felt like I could be consumed by the sorrow and heartache, but my faith was strengthened by the prayers and faith of our families, our friends, and our church communities. In Isaiah 43:2, it says "When you pass through the waters, I will be with you; and when you pass through the rivers, they will not sweep over you. When you walk through the fire, you will not be burned; the flames will not set you ablaze." TNIV BIBLE.

John and I were not swept away or set ablaze by this accident. We both thankfully had survived the ordeal of Johns motorcycle accident.

chapter 10

Hope and a Future

~

"For I know the plans I have for you declares the lord. Plans to prosper you and not to harm you. Plans to give you hope and a future."

Jeremiah 29:11

O ctober 10, 1986, our wedding day had finally arrived. It was fall, but it looked exactly like the beautiful summer day on July 5th, our original wedding date. The sky was beautifully blue without a cloud in sight, with a warm breeze, and it was a joyful day.

I felt like a princess in my beautiful sparkly white wedding dress. I wore my hair up, and my veil complimented the dress perfectly. As my bridesmaids were arriving for pictures, it was starting to feel real. Jennifer and my niece Carla were flower girls and looked angelic in their white dresses with peach satin sash and bows around their waists and flowers in their hair.

My sister Joyce was my maid of honor, and her son Danny was our adorable ring bearer in his little white tuxedo and his bright red hair.

I was so happy the wedding was finally real. I was truly ecstatic and had a smile plastered across my face. It didn't matter that as I was walking down the aisle, I noticed the flowers on the altar were not what I had ordered; I didn't care. John and I were there to make this commitment to become husband and wife, and hundreds of people were there to celebrate with us.

It was one of the happiest days of my life, and it seemed like it took several miracles for it to really happen.

We had a traditional Catholic Wedding, and even though we got married on a Friday at 5:00, the church was packed with our family and friends. Everyone was so happy that John had survived and recovered from his motorcycle accident, and they wanted to be there to celebrate with us.

After the mass, we walked down the aisle as husband and wife to greet our guests in the receiving line. Everyone was given a white or peach balloon to release up into the clear blue sky with best wishes for our future together.

Our wedding reception was pleasantly fun. The food, cake and cookies were great. John's mom, Lorraine, surprised us with a huge ice carving – a heart with love birds kissing on top. The caterer arranged all the cookies in hearts and carved birds out of apples. The D.J. was fantastic, and everyone, young and old, danced the night away.

It was a celebration of miracles. John and I had been through so much, and we felt so blessed to be celebrating this time with the people that had helped us through. It was a night to remember.

Since we got married on a Friday, we had Saturday to spend with our family to open wedding gifts. Then on Sunday the 12th, we took off for our honeymoon to Montego Bay, Jamaica.

I felt like I died and went to heaven. I had never seen sand so white or water so warm and turquoise. It looked like something from a postcard. The temperature was in the 90's every day, with crystal blue skies. Water skiing was included in our package, so we did that almost every day. The resort was a tropical paradise with palm trees, amazing swimming pools, and hot tubs under the stars. They had hammocks in the trees and beach volleyball. So much to do or not do anything and just relax and work on our tans.

The week flew by, and it was time to head back to reality. Even though Jamaica was fun, I missed Jennifer. I had quit my job at JoS. A. Bank to start working with John and his mom at Wahl Heating and Cooling. The day we got home from our honeymoon, I barely had my laundry started when Lorraine was knocking on the door to see if I wanted to come downstairs to the office and learn the bookkeeping job.

We lived in one of the apartments in the building above our Business. It was going to take some getting used to having very little separation from our work and home life. And unfortunately, we still had to deal with Lenny. He was still not seeing Jennifer, and I had to ride her to and from school. I also had to inform the school that under no circumstances was anyone other than John or I to pick Jennifer up from school. We were very protective because we never knew what to expect from Lenny.

Jennifer liked having her dog Chris around, the Siberian Husky, even though he was too strong for her to walk him. I could barely walk Chris because he was so brawny. To make matters worse, Chris was not a very good guard dog either.

One Monday morning, shortly after we were married, John and I walked down the steps from our apartment to start the day in the office, and to our surprise, our large front window had been shot out with a shotgun while we were asleep upstairs. Chris, our dog, apparently slept through it as well. There was broken glass all over the desks and the floor.

We called the police to file a report and let them know that the Magistrate had warned Lenny to stay away from us after the terroristic threats he had made about blowing John's head off. It was good that we had a police record of all the harassment and that the existing case made it possible for the police to finally go and arrest Lenny. He was not given bail based on the conditions surrounding the case. He was being held in jail until the hearing, which happened to be seven months later, and that meant he would be spending Christmas in jail. When the hearing finally arrived, we had little to keep him in jail. The main witness, that lived across the street, had moved to California and could not return for the hearing. Lenny was going to get out of jail, but our hope was that he learned a huge lesson. We were not playing games, and we wanted him to leave us alone. Lenny was so delusional he was telling the judge that he and I had been married, which was a complete lie. The judge told him none of what had happened previously mattered and told him to leave all of us alone and go through the courts if he wanted to see Jennifer.

I never did get any child support from him, nor did I want it at this point. We just wanted him to move on with his life and stop harassing us.

John and I made the decision to get a guard dog that would alert us to any danger, and we gave Chris to my sister Joyce who was a runner and loved having him. We got a pretty German Shepard named Lady. She was trained to attack on command. John also started always carrying a handgun with him for protection. I had constant nightmares that Lenny was going to try and kidnap Jennifer or kill John or me.

It was a very scary time but for the most part after Lenny got out of jail, he kept his distance. I think his time in jail made him realize we were not going to put up with him threatening us anymore. We were doing our best to protect each other and Jennifer and to hope and persevere and believe that one day we would not have to watch our backs all the time and be able to just live a peaceful life.

To help us with privacy and security, John and I started looking for our first home. I felt so good looking at houses. It was hard to live a private life when we were living above our business.

We were planning to wait until we found a house to get pregnant, but to our surprise, I was already pregnant. I was scared when I first found out I was pregnant because I had just had low back x-rays. I had told the x-ray technician there was no way I could be pregnant because I should not have been. I was having some spotting which didn't seem normal, and I was concerned about that as well. It was recommended that I go talk to genetic doctors about my concerns. I was afraid they would recommend that I terminate the pregnancy, and I knew I would not do that, so I never went. I was so worried about having had the x-rays and being pregnant that I cried for days. Then I prayed about all my fears surrounding the x-rays, and I turned it over to God.

I thought if something is wrong with this baby or pregnancy that I would either miscarry or live with whatever happens. I stopped worrying and started enjoying being pregnant. My Ob/Gyne did a sonogram as soon as it made sense, and everything was fine with the baby. Jennifer was now eight and so excited about me having another baby because she had repeatedly been mentioning that she really wanted a little brother or sister. It was such a blessing to be pregnant and be happily married; this was a very different experience for me.

We found our beautiful three-bedroom, 2 ½ bath home in a great suburb near Pittsburgh, with a great school district. It had room for John to build a home office for me to help take care of the rental property from home and a game room we could make into a 4th bedroom.

It was a red brick multi-level with white siding and slate blue shutters. It had a great big, flat backyard for the kids to play in with a wooded area behind us. It was perfect for us, and we were excited to move in.

We did not know if we were having a boy or a girl, but we were due in early December, and we wanted to get in the house by the fall. It was exhausting moving pregnant, but that is what we did. I was around seven months, and I remember not being able to move the next day; I was so wiped out. There were still a couple of months before baby Wahl was due to get a sweet nursery set up. We got dark wood furniture for the nursery and picked wallpaper and bedding with little boy bears, and little girl bears doing things like swinging on a swing. It was pastel colors, and I absolutely loved it. John's father, Bill, taught me how to hang wallpaper, and I was hooked. It was getting close to baby Wahl arriving, so I had to take a break.

In late November, two weeks early, our beautiful and healthy baby girl, Sarah, was born. We were over the moon. She had brown peach fuzz and brown eyes like her dad. She had the cutest little mouth, and I could not stop looking at her face.

Jennifer had taken the big sister class before the baby arrived, so she was super excited to see and hold her little sister, Sarah. She had wanted a little sister for so long, and now she was here.

Jennifer was adjusting well to her new school, but the School District was giving us a hard time about us not using the name on Jennifer's birth certificate. When Jennifer was born, I gave her my last name. However, when Lenny found out I did not give her his last name, he had a fit. He would not rest until I wrote to the State and notified them that there had been a mistake when filling out the documents in the hospital, and I requested that they correct the error and change her last name to his last name. When I got married, I registered Jennifer for school using my married name Wahl. It was all quite a mess. Some of her early school records even had my maiden name. I understood that we had to do something. I did not think Lenny would let John adopt Jennifer, but I thought we could get him to agree to a legal name change for her sake.

We hired an attorney and filed the petition to go to court for the legal name change. Lenny asked Jennifer if she wanted her name to be changed. By this point, she was nine years old and old enough to understand what was going on. When Jennifer said that she did want my last name, Lenny agreed to allow us to legally change her name to Wahl. He told me he could tell we were doing a great job raising her, and he was happy about that. He had finally stopped harassing us. I am not sure if that is because the past child support was building up in arrears. If I had made a big deal about the child support arrears, Lenny could have been arrested. I was happy he was leaving us alone, and we did not need or want the money. We were happy just to finally have peace in our lives.

In October of 1989, on the weekend of our third wedding anniversary, John and I had a family member stay with Jennifer and Sarah, so we could go away overnight. Sarah was almost one, and we had baby stuff in every room. The highchair, swing, walker, stroller, etc. Since we were in full baby mode, we discussed the possibility of trying for a boy over the weekend.

We had such a great time being away from work and the city in the scenic Laurel Mountains of Pennsylvania. And we did, in fact, succeed in our mission to conceive another child. We were all so excited about this pregnancy. It felt so nice to be celebrating and expecting this new baby with our family and friends. I had been through such drama in the past, and this was just a peaceful, happy feeling. That is, until the morning sickness kicked in.

I was sure we were having a boy because I had more morning sickness this time and was extremely tired all the time. I had never felt like that before when I was pregnant. This time we didn't want to wait to find out. We had a sonogram done on March 6[th,] and it confirmed that we were, in fact, having a baby boy. We were overjoyed.

We had to move Sarah out of the nursery and into a "big girl" bed. John and I made the game room into Jennifer's bedroom. We added built-in closets for clothes and a built-in desk to do her homework. Jennifer loved the big bedroom because she now had a TV in her bedroom.

I was due July 18th, but thankfully, David arrived in early July. He was healthy and happy, and even though he was two weeks early, he was 7pds, 12 ounces. He had chubby cheeks with big dimples, big brown eyes, and he always had a smile on his face.

I felt blessed to be able to be home with our children and manage the rental properties from my home office. But because John was building the heating and cooling business and doing most of the sales appointments, he worked a lot of evenings. As much as the idea of owning two businesses sounds promising, there are pros and cons of owning two businesses.

I spent many hours driving Jennifer to and from soccer practice and games with two babies in the car. Many nights the kids were already in bed by the time John got home from work, but he was always a good husband, father to our children and provider. When John would get home early, we would put Sarah and David in a double stroller, and the five of us would all go for a walk around our pretty suburban neighborhood. We had a tire swing and a swing set in our backyard, so the neighborhood kids would come over and play in our backyard. It was a great neighborhood for families.

John and I were truly blessed and felt Jeremiah 29:11 in our lives. The Lord had watched over us, protected us, and given us hope and a future.

chapter 11

Looking Back to Move Forward

~~~~

"If you must look back, do so forgivingly. If you must look forward, do so prayerfully. However, the wisest thing you can do is be present in the present... gratefully."

Maya Angelou

O n the outside, it looked like I had it all. A loving husband, three healthy children, a beautiful home, a fancy car, my health, nice clothes, jewelry, and luxury vacations. But I felt like I was living in a glass house. I was often afraid to answer the phone because I thought it could be bad news. I hated hearing and seeing police cars and ambulance sirens and lights. I tried to pretend I was fine. I went into perfection mode. I thought that if I, our home, and the kids looked perfect, then we must be the perfect happy family. I was driving myself crazy trying to keep that up. I had everything I ever wanted but was afraid that at any moment, it could all be taken away from me. I decided to seek the help of a therapist to try and help me figure out why I was afraid to be happy. It took me a long time to figure out what the heck was happening to me. I was referred to a therapist named Manny, who I swear was sent from above. This little man with an accent was kind and loving as he listened to me spill my heart out. I was struggling with some depression and started wondering why I could not enjoy all the wonderful gifts in my life.

All the previous physical and verbal abuse, two abortions, releasing a baby girl for adoption, the date rape and John's motorcycle accident and having to cancel our wedding were all still affecting me. Even going back to cheerleading and friends being taken away. It was all still there under the surface. I was suffering from post-traumatic stress, post-abortion syndrome and imposter syndrome and did not even realize it. Impostor Syndrome is a psychological occurrence in which an individual doubts their skills, talents or accomplishments and has a persistent internalized fear of being exposed as a fraud. That made total sense. Inside I was still the battered girl. I needed to let her go and finally accept who I had become. I was a new creation.

I had told John almost everything about my past when I met him, but I had never told him about the date rape. It had happened only a month before I met John, and I just buried it inside myself, but it needed to be addressed so I could really move on.

Manny told me I was living in my own hell, and we both agreed that I would tell John about the date rape. We also discussed that since I had no physical evidence and I could not legally proceed with any legal action against the rapist, that as far as I was concerned, my rapist no longer existed in my world. If I saw him anywhere, he did not exist. I did not want John to go after him or do anything to bring him into our lives. I was working on healing myself and forgiving him. I believe that to drug and rape someone, you must be really messed up. I started to feel sorry for my rapist as a person, and that helped me process what happened and move on. I only wish I would have pressed charges to spare other women the same experience with him because I am sure I am not the only woman he drugged and raped. Talking through what happened in the safety of the therapy office helped me process what happened to me, but I still had to tell my loving husband what had been bothering me for so long. We went into our bedroom and closed the door. I shared with him about that horrible night and the secret that had haunted me. He held me in his arms, and we cried together.

I mentioned earlier in this book one of my favorite quotes by Ralph Waldo Emmerson, "What lies behind us and what lies before us are tiny matters compared to what lies within us." I found this to be so true in my own life. I could no longer stuff things down inside of me that happened and expect to lead a happy, productive life. I had to look inside and deal with what I found there.

In my therapy with Manny, I started to examine my life. I started to understand that I was a minor, fourteen years young, when I met Lenny. I may have acted older and dressed older, but I was still fourteen. Having a child at fifteen made me "grow up" quickly, or should I say take on adult responsibilities quickly, but I was still fifteen. I was not equipped to handle the decisions I was making. I did the best I could with the situations I was in, along with my parents and family.

Working on forgiving myself and forgiving Lenny was a big part of healing. I realized that I could not change the past; I could only change how I dealt with it and focus on the present and the future. Forgiving Lenny for all the terrible things he said and did to me was going to take time, but I began praying for the healing of memories.

For years if Lenny's name came up, I would have terrible nightmares that he broke down the door and was in the house or coming after John or me or kidnapping Jennifer. I prayed for the healing of my dreams, and eventually, the nightmares stopped.

Manny helped me begin the journey of learning to love myself with all my regrets. We all make mistakes as we go through this life but what's important is what we learn from them. With Manny's help and my strong faith, I began to grow into a much happier and loving wife, mother, and person.

I was finally able to feel good about what I had survived and accomplished. I was able to enjoy my life without fear of it all being taken away at any moment. I also learned the blessings of gratitude. I now start each day by writing down at least five things I am grateful for in a journal. This simple act helps me focus on those positive things and then attract more positivity into my life. Some days my gratitude is a hot cup of coffee and simple things. Every day, I am grateful for my faith, my family, and my health.

Shortly after my sessions ended with Manny, he was diagnosed with pancreatic cancer. He did not live very long after he was diagnosed, only a couple of months. He had such a profound impact on my life, and I am eternally grateful to have gotten to know him as I got to know, love, and forgive myself. Rest in Peace, Manny M. I will never forget you and how much you helped me heal.

A good therapist is worth their weight in gold. If you choose to seek the help of a therapist, make sure you find someone you feel comfortable with. Manny and I had discussed that I always wanted to be honest with my children about the past, so when questions started coming up, I would know it was time to have some real conversations with my two youngest children.

Things were going well for our family, and I wanted to keep it that way. Sarah and David knew nothing of Lenny and the hell John, Jennifer, and I went through before they were born. Jennifer had the same last name as them, and we did not have any contact with Lenny, so all was good.

Then I found out that Lenny had been injured on an ironworking job. I was afraid that he would get a large settlement and pay off the large amount of child support that was owed, and want to start seeing Jennifer. Up until now, he had been leaving us alone because he did not want to go to jail for back child support. We had only done a legal name change, not an adoption. So once again, we sought legal advice, and we went for it. John wanted to adopt Jennifer, and she wanted him to adopt her. She was almost sixteen years old, but we wanted to make it official.

Our attorney notified Lenny to let him know that I would forgive all the child support that was in arrears if he allowed John to adopt Jennifer. By this point, it was well over $25,000. I did not want any money from him, just for this final step to be done so we no longer had to worry about him coming back into the picture.

On May 5th, 1994, my husband John legally became Jennifer's father even though he had taken on that role over ten years earlier when he fell in love with her at age five. He was the dad that taught her how to ride her bike and paid for her braces, and cheered her on to play saxophone and soccer. John had been Jennifer's dad for years, but it was now official.

It was about this time when Sarah and David started to ask questions about why Jennifer, their older sister, was in our wedding pictures. I had always promised myself I would be honest with my kids about the past. I began to explain as best I could without giving them too much information about what had happened before I met their dad.

I told them that before I met their dad, I met a man that I thought was a nice and good man, and we had Jennifer together. And then he turned out not to be a nice man.

Sarah said, "Is that the man that hurt you real bad?" I was in shock. I had no idea how she knew that other than she must have overheard a conversation. I told her "Yes" that he did hurt me really bad, and that is why Jennifer and I had to leave him.

Since I was already into the story, I decided to tell them about their other sister, the baby girl I released for adoption. I pulled out their little baby footprints from when they were born. I showed them their own footprints, and I showed them Jennifer's footprints. Then I pulled out the other footprints that belonged to their biological sister.

They looked really confused, and then Sarah covered her face and began to cry. She said, "Oh no, did she die?" and I said, "no, Sarah, she did not die." Now she and David were more confused but relieved. I explained to them, as I had explained to Jennifer so many years ago that at that time I could not take care of another baby. I did not have a job or a good husband. I had just gotten away from a really abusive man, and I wanted her to have a better life than I could offer her then. I wanted her to be safe.

I told them she was with a really good mom and dad and that someday maybe we would meet her. I told them that I was told they named her Anna (not her real name to maintain privacy). From then on, Sarah started writing in her little journal to her absent sister, Anna.

I did not know exactly where Anna was, but I believed with all my heart she was safe and well because Mrs. Duncan, who I admired and respected, had picked the family based on my requirements. I remembered the wonderful things Mrs. Duncan had told me about her adoptive mom having a bubbly, outgoing personality like mine and that I would love her. They had adopted a son first, and I was happy that she would have a sibling since I was happy to have brothers and sisters. I knew that the dad had a good job and that they had strong faith.

I still longed to know what she looked like, and I wondered about her life. Sometimes it would make me sad, and I would cry, but I always believed that one day we would meet, and I prayed for her and her family as I prayed for my family. Sometimes I would write letters to her that I could not mail. But it felt good to put the words on paper. I continued to pray that one day we would meet and be able to have some type of relationship.

We had both survived, and for that, I was grateful. I felt happy that I had broken the cycle of abuse. My children and I would no longer be subjected to that violence. I stood up for us and said enough, and left before it was too late. I needed to do what I did for all of us. My one wish is that I would have left sooner, but I did leave, and I am happy to be a survivor.

It would be many years before I would embark on the journey to connect with the daughter I had lovingly released for adoption back in 1984. I wanted to respect her and her family, and I thought that when she was an adult, I would look for her to see if she was interested in having some type of relationship. I had always longed to tell her why I was not able to raise her myself, even though I wanted so badly to keep her. I wanted her to be safe and in a stable environment. When she was born, I had no idea what the future held. I was just trying to survive.

My life had turned out better than I expected, and I wanted to know how things had gone for her. In 2009 she would be turning twenty-five, my other children were grown, and they and my husband were super supportive. We made the decision it was time for me to embark on the long-awaited search to find Anna and see if we could have some type of relationship after all these years. I had hoped and prayed that maybe she would have found me since I had left it open with the Adoption Agency, but I didn't even know if Anna knew that. So, my mission to find and reach out to Anna began.

chapter 12

Reunion Miracles

"There are two ways to live your life. One is though nothing is a miracle the other is as though everything is a miracle."

Albert Einstein

Who knew that Sarah's life would take us to California, where we found our first clues to finding Anna. God works in mysterious ways.

My daughter, Sarah, had gotten involved with the musicals starting in middle school, and I was asked to help with the hair, makeup, and costumes. I loved being involved behind the scenes, especially working with the students. This experience led me to pursue a desire I had for a long time to get my cosmetology license. I have always been good at braiding hair, updos and applying makeup, so I thought I would enjoy doing it professionally.

I started cosmetology school in September of 2006, the same year Sarah was a senior in high school and David was a junior. I graduated in June of 2007 and went back for my cosmetology teacher's license because they offered me a scholarship to do it. I did not want to teach at that point, I wanted to work in a salon, but I did complete the course because I did not know what I would want to do in the future. I finished both programs and proceeded to pass my State Board Tests for both Pennsylvania Licenses. It felt good to be working on something I always had an interest in, and I was proud I passed my State Board Tests the first time around, despite having been stressed out about both tests before taking them.

After her high school graduation, Sarah auditioned for an acting school called AMDA, short for the American Musical and Dramatic Academy, and was accepted. John and I have always supported our children in pursuing their dreams. We were happy that Sarah was pursuing her dream of acting professionally but heartbroken that her dream was leading her all the way to California. Sarah said the AMDA in California was more focused on film and television, so that is where she needed to go.

I had been blessed to be so involved in her life with the musicals, and I was devastated for her to be moving to the other side of the country. Sarah was so excited about it and had worked so hard at everything she did that John and I chose to support her decision, despite her being so far away, in a different time zone, three hours later than Pittsburgh time.

During the first summer break of 2008, Sarah had only been home for a couple of weeks because she spent most of the summer at a stage combat training in North Carolina, working on choreographing fight scenes for stunt work. When it was time for her to head back to LA, I went with her to help her gather her belongings she had stored with friends. We decided to make a trip of it and rent a car and drive to visit my cousin Lynn who lived in Coronado, California, right by San Diego.

While visiting with Lynn, she asked Sarah and me if we wanted to go to her Church with her on Sunday. At the time, I was a practicing Catholic, but Sarah and I were both open to other spiritual experiences. Lynn told us that when we walked into the building, ministers would ask if we wanted to be prayed over. And just as Lynn told us, as we entered, there were men and women ministers in white robes offering to pray over us. I sat down, and a male minister gently placed his hands on my head and began to pray.

I felt completely fine when I sat down, and then from deep inside me came intense feelings, and I started to cry. And I mean cry. I had tears streaming down my face. By the time he finished, I had cried off all my makeup, but I felt this strange sense of peace. The service was getting ready to start, so I hurried up and ran to the bathroom to fix up my makeup with what I had in my purse. I rushed back to sit with Sarah and Lynn as the ministers proceeded out to begin the service.

The very first minister that walked up to the pulpit to speak said when she was praying, she received a message for the woman in the white sun dress. Everyone in the place turned to see who she was referring to. It was me. I was the woman in the white dress. She said she had a vision that I had a hole in my heart. Not literally, but that I was looking for someone. I almost fell over. She said she had more to tell me, but she would prefer to discuss it in private after the service. My cousin Lynn turned to me in shock. She said, "they never do that." After the service, Mary, the minister, told me that she had a vision while praying that I was missing a child or someone from my table. Part of her vision was a child on a milk carton. I told her that I was looking for my daughter, but she wasn't missing like that. I told Mary I had released a daughter for adoption back in 1984 and that she was old enough to decide if she wanted to have a relationship or not, but I was having trouble finding her. I had many people praying about it for me, including my mom and my Aunt Beats. My Mom and Aunt Beats were my prayer warriors. Especially for the intention of finding Anna, but we needed a break.

Mary, the minister we were speaking with, told me that she worked in adoption and that she also had adopted a daughter named Anna. She told me she was going to help me find the daughter I gave birth to all those years ago. She said the attorney that did the adoption knows who her adoptive parents are. She said I needed to write three letters. One to the Attorney that did the adoption, asking him to give the second letter to my daughter's adoptive parents. That letter would be asking them to give the third and final letter to their daughter from her birth mom, me.

When I got home from California, I started working on the letters. It was not easy to know what to say in each of the letters, and it took some time to get them right, but I wrote them, then I mailed them to the Adoption Attorney, and I prayed and waited. The holidays of 2008 came and went, but I was still waiting on a response from the attorney to see if he would give my letters to Anna's parents and, eventually, get my letter to Anna. He was not answering or returning my phone calls. It was frustrating and disappointing.

Then one day in the spring of 2009, out of the blue, I met this private investigator while pumping gas. He liked my convertible. It was champagne gold with a black roof. I loved that car too. We struck up a conversation, and I told him I was looking for a daughter I released for adoption many years ago. I explained about the letters I had written to the adoption attorney, and my new P.I. friend agreed to help me since I still had not heard back from the adoption attorney.

When I came back to the office and told John the story about meeting this private investigator and what he said, John looked sort of shocked. We tried some other options since the letters had not worked, but we had not had any luck. Finally, in May of 2009 and after much persistence from me and my new Private Investigator, the attorney that had handled the adoption of Anna agreed to give my letters to her parents. One letter was to her parents and one letter was to Anna.

The Adoption Attorney wanted the letter written so Anna would go through the adoption agency or him and not have her contact me directly. I agreed to rewrite the letters and mail them back to him. I sent the letters and once again began waiting. Waiting and praying for a response. It had been almost twenty-five years of wondering. So many questions and so much emotion. I guess it was a blessing that I was always so busy with two businesses, two houses and a family. It helped to keep my mind occupied.

On June 9th, I received an unexpected phone call from Carol, the Director of Genesis of Pittsburgh, the adoption agency that had handled the adoption twenty-five years ago. She was calling to let me know that Anna's parents had read my letter and that they had agreed to give her my letter. They were driving out of state for her twenty-fifth birthday, which was coming up at the end of the month. All my efforts were finally paying off. I had been hoping and praying since the day I had to let her go to finally find out more about my daughter, and it was finally happening. The date of June 9th was quite ironic. June 9th of 1986 was the day I had received the disturbing phone call about my then fiancé John's terrible motorcycle accident, really bad news. Now, I got wonderful news on June 9th. I just found it such a strange coincidence that I had two life-changing phone calls on June 9th, one terrible and one wonderful.

It would be several more months before I had any further correspondence. In September, I received another phone call from Carol at Genesis. She informed me that Anna had read my letter and that she had written back to me. She said I should have the letter any day. This was so exciting because it was going to be the first time I had ever heard from her. I could not wait to read her letter. Her letter was dated Sept. 24, 2009, but it didn't arrive until the beginning of October. It felt like an eternity because I knew it was coming and had been waiting for so long.

The good news she shared was that she had the happy and safe childhood that I wanted her to have. She had great parents and had gone to great schools. She played piano and soccer and got to graduate college. She was a teacher and was happily married and expecting their first child. She ended the letter by stating that someday she wanted to meet me and my family and get to know them too. But she was a little overwhelmed and that for now, wanted to communicate by writing letters to get to know each other. I was so happy to finally hear from her and relieved to know she had a happy life. I was fine with taking it slow, but I still did not know what she looked like as an adult. I guess deep down, I was hoping she would have included a photo with her letter. I had no idea what she looked like because the last time I saw her, she was two days old.

When I wrote back to Anna, I included a couple of photos so she could see what I looked like. We continued writing to each other, but we were taking it slow. Mainly because Anna and her husband, Jeremy, had just welcomed their new baby boy Michael in

November of 2009, and I know what it is like having a newborn. You need to learn a whole new routine, and getting rest when the baby is sleeping is important. I know in one of my letters, I provided my phone number and let her know that it was fine to call me whenever she was ready. There is no road map on how to proceed with building a relationship, especially since we lived in different states and she was a brand-new mom. We were taking it slow.

In December 2009, I started my new job in a busy, high-end Salon, and I was super excited. I was still a Landlord, but it was good for me to be doing something I enjoyed. At this salon, you need to start out assisting the senior stylists and the owner, but I was OK with that since I had started my hair stylist position later in life, and I wanted to continue to learn.

On Saturday, July 24th, 2010, I was at the Salon where I was working and had just taken a lunch break when my phone rang. I was surprised to hear the voice on the other end of the phone say, "Hello, this is Anna." I was so happy that tears of joy ran down my cheeks. I went outside and sat on the steps, and we talked for as long as I could at work. We exchanged email addresses, and she promised to send pictures of her and her family, including baby Michael. It was one of the happiest days of my life. To finally be able to share information with each other about our lives and know that I would finally get to see pictures of what she looks like and see pictures of her family and her baby.

When I got home, there were several emails with all kinds of pictures. Some from college, her wedding and even her honeymoon. John and I and our kids were thrilled to finally get to see her and know more about her. She looked so much like Jennifer, only with blue eyes and lighter brown hair. She had dimples like me, and she looked so happy. It was also nice to see photos of her husband, baby, her parents, and some of her college friends. I could not have been happier.

We continued to have phone conversations and started making plans to meet in person when she was home for Thanksgiving. What a difference a year makes. A year ago, we had never even spoken to each other, and now we were planning to meet in person; it was an exciting time.

Our reunion was finally happening. On Monday, November 22nd, 2010, Anna and I were being reunited. We arranged to meet at the school and Church she had attended growing up and was later married in. We met outside in a garden where there is a life-size statue of the Blessed Mother, Mary. It was quite appropriate that we met there because many rosaries had been prayed for this moment to be taking place. The fact that we both had survived the abuse and that we were meeting was a huge blessing and a miracle of how it all came to be.

We hugged each other and sat and talked like two old friends. We had a lifetime of things we wanted to share. One of the first things she said to me was, "You're so pretty." I think that was the first time I realized that once she knew she was adopted, she probably always wondered what I looked like, just like I wondered what she looked like. She knew she was adopted, and she and her mom sometimes would talk about me. But it was great to finally get to see each other in person. Anna looks a lot like her biological father but with my light brown hair and blue eyes. Jennifer looks more like me, with his dark brown hair and hazel eyes.

I almost felt like I was in a dream because I was so happy. I gave Anna the 14Kt gold crucifix that was a gift to me the day I had her. My friends gave it to me in the hospital. I wanted her to have it now. She gave me a beautiful hanging blessed mother ornament as a gift and then another unexpected surprise. She was pregnant with her second child. I could not have been happier for her and her entire family. I know how much I loved having brothers and sisters. We went to get some lunch and talked for hours. Anna was sweet, funny, and smart, and I really enjoyed our conversations. She asked me if I wanted to see where she grew up, and of course, I said, "yes."

She was driving her mom's car, and we drove past the house she grew up in. I was so shocked when I saw the house because it looked so similar to my first home. It was a red brick, split level with white siding and blue shutters, just like our house. The other crazy part was that she lived less than two miles and only a drive of four minutes away for the five years I lived in that home. It might as well have been on the other side of the world because I had no idea she lived there. I knew what county the family that had adopted her lived in, but I did not realize how close it was to me. I asked Anna if she wanted to see our first house where I had lived by her, and she said she did.

When we moved to our first home, we were technically within the boundary to go to the same Church that Anna and her family attended. But my husband and I really liked the Pastor at a different church close by, so we chose to go there instead. How crazy is that? We almost ended up at the same church as her family. I wonder if I would have figured out who she was from seeing Anna and her family at church. All I can say is that it must not have been meant to be.

We had spent several hours together, but she had to get back to her baby. The time we spent together was such a blessing. I did not know what the future would look like yet because she did not want to hurt her parents, and she was not ready to meet any other family members yet, so we agreed to continue to proceed slowly.

In June 2011, Anna had her second healthy baby boy, Christopher. It was so amazing to be communicating with her and get to see pictures of the baby. We continued to talk on the phone when we could, but that was not always easy with a newborn and a toddler, but we talked when we could.

The next time Anna was in town, she brought Michael and Christopher to lunch with us. I got to hold the baby, Christopher, and that was amazing. I cannot express to you the joy that I felt in my heart seeing these boys in person. Every struggle I went through to have Anna was worth it!

The next time Anna and I met up, her mom watched the boys so she could have a little break, and we had lunch that lasted for three hours. We had not seen each other in way too long, and we had so much to catch up on, including that she was expecting another baby in May of 2016.

I don't get to talk with Anna as often as I would like because she is busy raising a family, and we don't get to see each other often because she lives in another state. But I am super happy to be working on building our relationship, and that is awesome! We had talked a little about her biological father, and I was glad we did. I made sure to tell Anna that I had loved her father and that, over the years, I had forgiven him.

That made sharing the unexpected news that Lenny passed away on Saturday, September 3rd, 2016, at the age of fifty-seven easier. She had never met him, but he was her biological father, and I thought she had the right to know. When I heard the news of Lenny's passing, I was not surprised. I was surprised, based on his rough lifestyle, that he lived to age fifty-seven. I felt multiple emotions. Lenny had not harassed us in many years, but I did feel a little sense of relief that there was finally no possibility of having to deal with him ever again. We had lived in fear for so many years, and it was finally over.

A couple of years before he passed away, Lenny had called me at our heating & cooling business to make amends. He wanted to thank John and me for doing such a great job raising Jennifer. He said he had gotten clean and sober and was working in addiction counseling about an hour or so outside of Pittsburgh. I was happy for him that he finally found some peace in this world.

Jennifer and I talked about his passing, and we both pretty much felt the same way. Some relief and peace and a small amount of sadness for him.

I had long since forgiven him for all the pain he had caused. In fact, at this point in my life, I felt sorry for him and all the pain he had in his life before I met him and all that he missed out on in his life that could have been if he had not been so abusive. I was able to pray for him that his soul would be able to finally rest in peace. It took many, many years for me to get to this place of forgiveness. I was happy I finally had peace inside of me.

As John and I were coming up on our 30th wedding anniversary in October of 2016, we wanted to do something special. We renewed our wedding vows at the church where we were married, St. Catherine of Sienna, with our adult children present, Sarah, via skype from California. This was a great experience for us to stand with each other before God and recommit to our marriage. We had been through some rough times, but we worked them, and are stronger together because of all of it.

After the evening celebration, we headed out on a road trip in our 2015 Crystal Red Corvette, our dream car! One of the blessings of this trip was that John and I were going to stop and visit Anna, her husband, and their three boys. I was so excited to see Anna again and meet Jeremy, her husband. I had only met her two older boys once, and they were toddlers then. My husband, John, had not met any of them, so we were filled with anticipation. We were on the road, and I was so happy that I felt like my heart was going to leap out of my chest.

It was such a huge blessing to be spending time with Anna, her husband, and the boys. Michael and Christopher were six and five at the time, and they loved our Corvette. We went outside and let them get in the car and check it out. They had a great time. Michael said he was going to have a Corvette when he grew up. We brought them each a toy Corvette, and they had a great time with those too. They showed us their playroom and all the things they had built with their legos. The boys were filled with energy, and I couldn't take my eyes off them.

We sat and talked and looked at Anna's wedding photos, and then we all sat down for dinner. When the baby was fussing, I offered to rock him while everyone finished eating, and he fell asleep in my arms. I can honestly say this was one of the best days of my life. I looked at Anna and Jeremy and how happy they were, and I looked at these adorable little boys and was proud of the decision I had made all those years earlier to fight for her life.

Looking back on being unexpectedly pregnant at nineteen and already have a four year old daughter while being in an extremely abusive relationship with their father, I had no idea how we were going to survive with him, and finally, I realized we weren't. We would only survive if we got away from him before it was too late.

Because of my faith in God, the support of my amazing family and some good friends, we survived. Many abused women and their babies don't survive. Looking back, I realize I should have left sooner. There were red flags flying in my face. I now know that if you need the police or others to protect you from your boyfriend or husband, you need to leave. But back then, I thought I could fix him. He kept saying he would change, that "IT," the abuse, would never happen again. I could not fix him, despite my efforts, and he was not changing. I had to protect myself and my children, and that is what I did.

As my husband, John and I were driving home, I thanked God for that special day with Anna, Jeremy, and the boys. I was also thankful that I chose love and life over fear all those years ago. Otherwise, my birth daughter and those three little boys would not be alive. I was filled with gratitude that Anna had such a loving and caring husband and father for her and their sons.

Coincidence or God-Incidence.

And then what I call a God-incidence happened at a TJ-MAX of all places. It was early in May of 2017, and I was pushing my cart through the aisles of the silk plant area when I saw a woman with dark hair and rosy cheeks that caught my eye. I did not want to stare, but she resembled the photo of Anna's Mom I saw when we were looking at photo albums of Anna's wedding. I did not know what to do, but I did not want to stare at her. I had a gut feeling it was Anna's Mom; I just wasn't certain.

In a bit of a panic, I pushed my cart into the dressing room and proceeded to try on the two yellow shirts that were in my cart. I took a couple of deep breaths and said a little prayer. Something like, "Lord, if that is Anna's Mom, and we are supposed to meet, I will see her again when I go to check out of the store." I got dressed and walked through the store to the cash register area to pay for purchases. I did not see her and was getting ready to leave the store when I realized that I forgot to get the pink Himalayan salt I came for. I turned around and headed straight for that area of the store, and I almost literally ran into her. Our eyes met, and she said, "hello," and I said, "hello, are you Michelle?" She looked at me kind of in shock and said, "how do you know that?" I said, "I am Sharon Wahl." At that point, we both just put our arms up and embraced in a tearful hug right in the store. I asked if it was okay if we talked for a minute, and she said "absolutely". It was quite surreal. I was standing in the store talking to the woman who raised Anna. We were both her moms, and yet it was quite nice. I thanked her for doing such a great job raising Anna to be the woman she is. She thanked me for the sacrifice I made and for giving her the opportunity to have a daughter and be her mom and now a grandmother. We shared that we had both prayed for each other over the years. That made me feel good inside to know that she prayed for me.

We stood and talked about our families for about twenty minutes. I wanted to exchange contact information in case we ever wanted to talk again, but I could not find any of my business cards with my phone number. I was happily surprised when Michelle reached out her hand with one of her cards with her contact information. She did not have to do that. I think we were both kind of in shock about meeting so unexpectedly. Now, the more I think about it, I am kind of surprised we never met before because we live in the same area. I believe it was meant to be that day.

We followed up our meeting with an email shortly after our initial meeting, and we text periodically on Mother's Day to share our gratitude for the gift of life and our shared bond with Anna and her family.

I did not plan on meeting Michelle that day, and I have no idea what the future looks like. God knows, and that is fine with me. I find things seem to work out better when I just trust in the process.

I had no idea that Sarah moving to California and us going to my cousin's Church was going to be a huge part of the puzzle of finding Anna. Who knew that the man I was talking to while pumping my gasoline would turn out to be a Private Investigator? I cannot even remember his name, but he was the person that influenced the Adoption Attorney to finally give Anna's parents my letters. Who knew I would casually meet Anna's Mom at a local store? Who knew all these pieces would come together? God knew!

Conclusion

A Unique Perspective

"Alone we can do so little; together we can do so much."

Helen Keller

I am truly happy to be alive, and I feel blessed beyond measure. Sometimes I wonder why I survived so many dangerous experiences.

I believe it was to write and tell my story because of my unique perspective.

Several years ago, I worked as part of a team presenting a talk on a Women's Retreat. My talk was called "Knowing God Through Knowing Myself," and my talk was the first talk of the retreat.

The leader of the retreat began by reading a prayer / poem aloud to the group. It was shared to allow the participants to begin to let their guard down and start to get real with themselves and where they were in their lives. I don't remember all of it but what I will never forget is what happened as she read the words aloud. It talked about how we all walk around with invisible masks on, wearing fake smiles on the outside when on the inside, we are not ok. Sometimes the masks are humor to cover pain or aggression or perfectionism to hide fear, etcetera. You get the point. She then let everyone know they were in a safe space and that it was ok and even helpful if we, in confidence, were open and share with each other over the course of the weekend to allow some healing to take place. The ladies were asked to stand if comfortable if any of them had ever experienced any of the following; a miscarriage or inability to have children, anyone ever sexually assaulted, had an abortion, adopted a child or released a child for adoption, been through a divorce or lost a child to murder, addiction or an accident, been a single parent, had a child come out as gay, anyone widowed, happily married, a mom, grandmother or aunt. There may have been other things on the list, but the idea is that we have so much in common as women and that if we share our truths, our trials, and triumphs, it can help someone else. By the time she finished reading, all the ladies were standing. It was liberating to look around and realize we are not alone in our joys and struggles as women, wives, and mothers.

As I was walking to the podium, a song was being played that I had chosen by Plumb called "Need You Now." The words were perfect for my talk. I am not going to write out all the lyrics, but it starts out with, "Everybody's got a story to tell, and everybody's got a wound to be healed. I want to believe there's beauty here, 'cause oh I get so tired of holding on, I can't let go, I can't move on, I want to believe there's meaning here. How many times have you heard me cry out "God please take this," how many times have you given me strength to just keep breathing, oh I need you, God I need you now. Standing on a road I didn't plan, wondering how I got to where I am, I trying to hear that still small voice, I'm trying to hear above the noise, how many times have you heard me cry out "God please take this," how many times have you given me strength to just keep breathing, Oh I need you, God, I need you now."

There are more verses to the song, but this song spoke to where I was so many times in my life and related to the talk I was about to give on that retreat. I had made a mess of my life so many times, and I thank God, My Higher Power, for always being there when I cried out for help. My talk was about my journey of coming to know God in a deeply personal way while growing to know myself as a person and woman through the trials and joys of life. I share all of this because I believe as women, we are the ones capable of breaking the cycle of abuse and destruction.

I never expected to be pregnant at fourteen and have my first child at fifteen. It was not easy being a teenage mom, but I would do it all again to have such an amazing daughter. I would have preferred to have had my first child as an adult, but that is not how it happened. In fact, Jennifer said she remembered my 21st birthday; she would have been six years old. I simply cannot imagine my life without Jennifer. She has been such a powerful force in my life.

I never expected to be in an abusive relationship and have him coerce and terrify me into having two abortions. Those decisions were made from fear and ignorance, and I will regret them for as long as I live.

I never expected to have a beautiful, healthy baby girl and release her for adoption. Leaving the hospital without my baby was like leaving a part of my body and soul behind and trusting someone else to care for her as I would. I did trust in the family I picked and the amazing woman who helped me pick them. To say it was difficult would be an understatement, but it was a choice that I could live with, and so could she. The choice to release my child for adoption was made from love, not fear.

Giving birth to my daughter, Sarah, and son, David, with my husband, John, was a completely different experience than my pregnancies with an abusive man. They were much more joyful pregnancies and birth experiences. I am grateful to have had the opportunity to have those experiences as well. I am truly amazed at the whole process of being able to grow a person, feel life, give birth and then be able to produce milk to feed them. Being able to give birth to all my children is a gift. They have all influenced me, inspired me, and they have made me a better version of myself.

After my talk on that retreat, "Knowing God through Knowing Myself," I had women approach me and share things with me that they had never told anyone before. They felt such relief knowing they were not alone. They had committed to seeking help through therapy to deal with the things they had hidden inside themselves for so long, just like I did. A year later, I worked another retreat with one of those women, and she said my honesty and sharing my story helped her finally get the help she needed. She was working with a women's group and feeling like a new person. Just like the "Me Too" movement, we are more powerful when we stand together.

I hope and pray that something in my crazy story helps give you hope and healing.

May God bless your journey to finding inner peace, joy, love, and the best version of yourself.

1 Corinthians 13:13 AND NOW THESE THREE REMAIN: FAITH, HOPE AND LOVE. BUT THE GREATEST OF THESE IS LOVE.

RESOURCES

* **National Domestic Abuse Hotline And Website:**
    Get Help 24/7 Call: 1-800-799-Safe (7233) Or
    Thehotline.Org

* **Rainn- Rape, Abuse, Incest National Network:**
    Get Help 24/7 Call 1-800-656-Hope (4673)
    Or Rainn.Org

* **Unplanned Pregnancy**
    Nrlc.Org – National Right To Life
    Optionline.Org 1-800-712-Help (4357)
    Standupgirl.Com 24/7

* **Mom In Crisis:**
    Call 833-477-6588
    Proloveministries.Org

* **National Post Abortion Helpline:**
    24/7 866-721-7881 Or H3helpline.Org
    Help Hope Healing

There is Always Hope and Help Available.

Please Seek Help and Know You Are Not Alone.

CPSIA information can be obtained
at www.ICGtesting.com
Printed in the USA
LVHW010003090623
749248LV00013B/876